CATALYTIC EXPERIENCES

PERSUADING SCIENTISTS AND CLINICIANS
WITH EFFECTIVE DIGITAL MARKETING

HAMID GHANADAN

LINUS|PRESS
A Division of The Linus Group, Inc.
5900 Hollis Street, Suite R1
Emeryville, CA 94608
www.thelinusgroup.com

Copyright ©2016 The Linus Group, Inc.
All Rights Reserved

Editor: Deborah Ager
Copyeditor: Bernadette Geyer
Cover Design and Interior Composition: Rikki Campbell Ogden / pixiedesign, llc

Printed in the United States of America
First Edition: 2016
Library of Congress Control Number: 2016941910
ISBN: 978-0-9975237-0-6

CATALYTIC EXPERIENCES

PERSUADING SCIENTISTS AND CLINICIANS WITH EFFECTIVE DIGITAL MARKETING

HAMID GHANADAN

To morning whispers

TABLE OF CONTENTS

PART ONE: Synthesis

3 INTRODUCTION
A Central Question
Does Your Marketing Work?

7 CHAPTER 1
This Is Your Audience's Brain on Technology
How Scientists and Clinicians Consume Information

23 CHAPTER 2
The Digital Evolution of Marketing Science and Healthcare
A Guide to Developing Effective Marketing in the New Digital Era

41 CHAPTER 3
The Model Model
Situating the Content-Centric Model Among Other Sales and Marketing Models

PART TWO: Stories

61 CHAPTER 4
The New Art of Western Blotting— GE Healthcare Life Sciences
Launching a New Product in a Crowded Market

83   CHAPTER 5
     We Are All Connected—Invitae
     Activating a Brand

107 CHAPTER 6
     Passion in Science—New England Biolabs
     Solidifying a Company's Connection to New Audiences

127 CHAPTER 7
     A Better Tip—Biotix
     Creating a Digital Infrastructure to Drive the Audience's Decision Journey

149 CLOSING
     A New Question
     What Lies Beyond the Horizon?

PART ONE:
Synthesis

Several fundamental differences in the digital landscape are rendering traditional marketing communications strategies ineffective. At first glance, the digital landscape is built on quicksand. By the time we as marketers adapt to new communications media and technologies, they change. As new technologies and modalities cause the old ones to become obsolete, scientists and clinicians stop paying attention, the world becomes enamored by new scenery—only to shift again a few short months later.

There is a longer view, however. We should not chase technologies or trends. Instead, we need to focus on the changing nature of our audience and consider their landscape. Only then can we develop highly effective digital marketing strategies that drive significant results today and put us on a virtuous cycle to gain even more visibility in the future.

In Part One of this book, I provide a tour of three key dynamics that affect how scientists and clinicians access and consume information and engage with marketing content. I then situate these shifts within the structure of the traditional marketing framework and create a path for evolution toward a highly effective digital marketing practice. As you will see, to succeed, you need to develop a framework for how to construct your messaging strategy. Finally, I review the Content-Centric Model for Marketing Science and Healthcare—the strategic framework for the buying journey of scientists and clinicians—and compare it with three other popular models for sales, marketing and branding.

By providing a synthesis of the digital landscape for scientists and clinicians, creating a path for evolution of marketing practices and situating the strategic framework for developing the right kinds of content, nested in optimal user experiences, you will have a clear view of the digital methods used to orchestrate effective marketing initiatives.

INTRODUCTION

A Central Question

Does Your Marketing Work?

I was ushered to a stark-white conference room with approximately 100 modern chairs, all lined up in neat rows with perfect precision. The receptionist offered me a cup of coffee while I set up for my presentation. Since it was 8:00AM in Germany and nine time zones ahead of my own body clock, I asked for two cups.

Soon, the crowd entered and took their seats. After a kind introduction from the global vice president of marketing at the hosting company, I began my presentation to describe how scientists, clinicians and technically trained professionals tend to make decisions and how we can more easily persuade them by satisfying their needs at each stage of their natural decision-making journey. As my talk progressed and I shared examples of the models, I could tell there would be numerous questions. When I concluded, several hands rose.

Questions are always my favorite part of giving a talk. Every question is informative, challenging and fun, and I learn so much with each interaction. We were having a nice discussion. Then a question came from the back of the room, and it would prove to be the most difficult question I had yet to receive about my work.

The scientist-turned-marketer asked: "I totally agree with your thesis and I find your model rational and compelling. But you have activated the skeptical scientist in me. If everyone reads your book and every science and medical company uses the Content-Centric Model for Marketing Science and Healthcare, will it still work?"

Indeed, this is a central question.

In my first book—*Persuading Scientists*—I presented the industry with a model for how scientists and clinicians make decisions and the specific classes of content that marketers should create to maximize the efficacy of their marketing efforts. The model presented in the book is inherent to the way scientists and clinicians tend to think and make decisions. Unlike novel technologies or 'tricks' that lose their efficacy over time, the Content-Centric Model for Marketing Science and Healthcare is a framework that allows marketers to search for their own insights, apply their own creative thinking and develop a myriad of ways to create unique strategies and meet their goals. Applied correctly, strategies will not lose their efficacy in the market irrespective of how many other companies adopt the model.

Since *Persuading Scientists* was published in 2012, we have surveyed thousands of scientists, clinicians and technical professionals, and have spoken with them through in-depth interviews during the course of our work at The Linus Group. We have also annually benchmarked the state of marketing in scientific, medical and other related technical industries to assess the industry's collective view on marketing practices.

Interestingly, the views of audiences and the marketers who try to connect with them are largely at odds with one another. But in this divide between how scientific and technical audiences behave and the rise of marketing and communications technologies lies a considerable opportunity to create more meaningful connections between companies and their audiences. By evolving the information that we as marketers produce through our marketing and communications efforts to match what our audiences want to engage in, we can effectively bridge the divide that separates us from our customers.

This book details the implementation of marketing strategies without chasing technologies or fads. I will first explore the intersection of the dynamics I have observed from audiences—scientists, clinicians and engineers—with our clients' current marketing practices and changes in communications technologies that impact how we relate, connect and do business. I then provide three key ingredients that are required for you to effectively execute digital marketing initiatives today while setting a foundation that will continue to pay dividends in the future as technologies shift.

CHAPTER 1

This Is Your Audience's Brain on Technology

How Scientists and Clinicians Consume Information

SYNOPSIS

The speed with which communications technologies have changed in the last decade has impacted how scientists, clinicians and technical audiences consume information and, as a result, make decisions. Therefore, anyone in the business of persuading scientists and clinicians needs to understand these changes in order to build a forward-looking commercialization strategy.

In this chapter, I review three key dynamics shaping how our audiences are changing their habits. I then synthesize these dynamics to create a picture of the near future and determine the necessary components of a successful marketing practice.

Throughout this chapter, I explore the following topics:

- Changes in how scientists engage in traditional marketing channels
- The mainstream embrace of social media and social communications technologies
- The concept of mobility and its effect on the traditional purchasing funnel
- How search engines are changing the types of content they consider as important
- The increasing skepticism of scientists as a result of the content explosion

This review of the digital landscape will serve as a basis for correctly and fully leveraging the principles of the Content-Centric Model for Marketing Science and Healthcare to maximize whatever marketing initiatives you need to accomplish.

OUT WITH THE TRADITIONAL

What is the relationship between privacy and celebrity? You may think this is an obtuse question, but consider how your audiences act on a daily basis. On the one hand, they are more protective of their privacy than ever before when it comes to their relationship with companies. At the same time, they are posting intimate details about their work and lives on social media sites.

The mainstream adoption of social media has utterly changed the way we communicate as a society, as peers, friends, colleagues and businesses. These communications have become so deeply engrained in our cultural norms that they have broken our expectations of traditional communications modalities.

The Linus Group engages in market research with thousands of scientists, doctors, nurses and engineers[1] on an annual basis and has observed key dynamics shaping how scientists engage with content. Increasingly,

1. Content explosion drives them to reject traditional media but embrace social media;
2. Mobility changes how they consume content;
3. They are skeptical of big business.

Due to these dynamics, scientific and medical marketers need to overhaul their marketing practices. Let us discuss the implications of these dynamics on marketing science and healthcare.

---

[1] For ease and editorial brevity, I refer collectively to all audiences within the science and medical industries as "scientists." This term, along with the models and frameworks presented in this book, applies equally as effectively to all audiences within these industries, including business decision-makers.

1. CONTENT EXPLOSION DRIVES SCIENTISTS TO REJECT TRADITIONAL MEDIA BUT EMBRACE SOCIAL MEDIA

Content is currency in science, medicine and engineering. These technical professionals produce and consume a tremendous amount of information as a central part of their vocation, and available content options continue to increase at a fast rate. The proliferation of scholarly publications, along with the need to keep up with the latest discoveries and standard practices, is overwhelming scientists and clinicians into silence—especially in the traditional media channels—resulting in an immunity to traditional marketing attempts.

Consider the growth in scholarly publications. In PubMed—a repository hosted by the National Institutes of Health—which indexes all biomedical publications, the number of annual publications indexed has doubled in the last 20 years and continues to grow at 5% per year. Any scientist in a biomedical field needs to stay current with the latest publications, yet there is more content than ever before to read and comprehend.

Scientists spend more time searching, more time sifting, and more time trying to make sure they are not missing something that is important to them. All of this takes time and attention away from all other sources of content.

Attendance at Major Trade Shows Continues to Decline

Scientists traditionally engaged with one another, as well as with content, at trade shows. The attendance at many major scientific and technical trade shows is flat or declining, rendering trade shows less effective in reaching audiences. Consider the number of attendees for two major trade shows in the past nine years, one in analytical sciences (Figure 01.01) that has seen significant declines, and the other in a discipline of biological science (Figure 01.02) that has plateaued in growth.

Although trade shows are a cornerstone of marketing in science and healthcare, the exact method for how to measure their effectiveness remains under debate. Points of view about how to measure the effectiveness of trade shows range

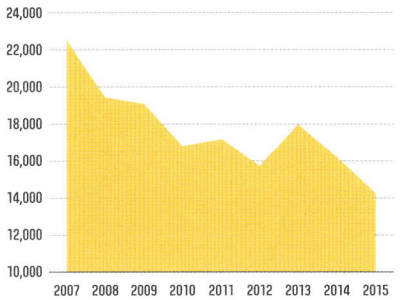
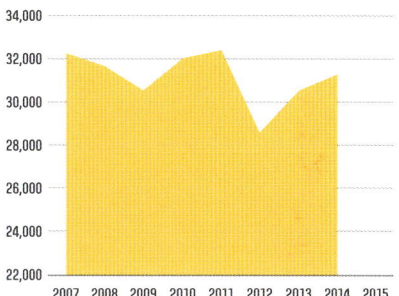

FIGURE 01.01 The total attendees reported from a major trade show focusing on the analytical sciences shows fairly steady and significant declines over the past 9 years. *(Synthesized from various sources.)*

FIGURE 01.02 Even in growing scientific fields, such as several disciplines within biological sciences, trade show attendance seems to have crested. *(Data published by hosting society.)*

from comparing them to other marketing channels (e.g., number of new leads acquired) to sales metrics (e.g., value of first-time meeting with a prospect[2]).

While sharing a taxi to the airport with a scientist after a major conference, I used the opportunity to gain anecdotal market intelligence and asked him about his experience at the conference. He noted that he was returning home after attending less than two days of the four-day conference. He mentioned that he had packed those two days with talks, poster sessions and meetings with colleagues during his short stay. "That's how everyone does it in conferences these days. No one stays the entire time. No one mills around or walks around. Who has the time?" I took special note of the lack of time for walking the trade show floor in his agenda. Even if a trade show does have healthy attendance, participants are more bombarded with content, making it more difficult than ever to grab their attention.

Median Email Open Rates Are Insufficient

In the olden days when life was much simpler, marketers paid publishers to carry and deliver their messages to audiences. In this fair and equitable contract,

---

[2] C. Porter. "The Value of Visitors." *Exhibitor Magazine*, January 2012, pg 40. Accessed online on October 25, 2015, at www.exhibitoronline.com/topics/article.asp?ID=1053.

publishers captured the attention of target audiences through interesting content, and marketers footed the bill with ads.

Then one day, marketers got wise. Since the early 2000s, marketers in science and medical industries have relied heavily on email to deliver their messages directly to their audiences, because this medium promised a more efficient and effective means of communication. "Why continue supporting intermediaries, when we can reach our audiences directly?" was the collective question being asked as advertising budgets were slashed in favor of upgrading contact relationship management (CRM) software and marketing automation solutions.

This trend continued until we, as marketers, tried it and saw just how difficult it was to generate real, lasting interest. The median email open rate reveals that fewer than 17% of email recipients open a mass email across all industries,[3] and though we see slightly higher open rates in the healthcare and scientific industries, on average, median click-through rates—the percentage of people who click on the call to action in an email message—only range from 1% to 3%. Finally, our own survey of science marketers reveals our collective view that email marketing is not going to become more effective in the future, with 69% of marketers either negative or neutral about their outlook on increased effectiveness of email marketing in the coming years.[4]

Due to these low open rates, we can no longer rely on the efficiency and effectiveness of email. We used to think different content would change these open rates and appreciated it as a lower-cost channel. However, we have learned audiences do not want to receive these emails in the first place.

When I give a speech, I sometimes ask the audience, "How many of you would like to receive more emails in your inbox?" No one raises a hand. Then, I ask, "How many of you would like to receive more *marketing* emails in your inbox?" Everyone laughs. And then the audience squirms a little with the realization of

---

[3]2014 SilverPop Email Marketing Metrics Benchmark Study. Accessed online on October 27, 2015, at www.silverpop.com/marketing-resources/white-papers/all/2014/email-metrics-benchmark-study-2014/.
[4]The Linus Group Survey of Life Science Marketers. Data available at www.thelinusgroup.com/CatalyticExperiences/Supplements.

our profession's dependency on a medium that we know to be undesirable and increasingly ineffective.

Every day, email bombards us. Only the most important of these messages will be opened and remembered. Marketing emails rarely fall into this category of being the most important. This societal trend extends into the scientific industry.

Banner Advertising Clicks Remain Steady

In advertising, especially for display and banner ads, there rarely exists a good way to measure results. Click-through rates (CTR) do not completely provide the full potential effect of advertising, but they are the most quantitative metric this medium offers. Banner and display CTR hovers between 0.06% and 0.1% according to DoubleClick.[5] In other words, only 6 out of every 10,000 impressions result in a click.

I do not advocate that the only measure of display advertising is click-through rates. Advertising works in psychological ways that should not be reduced to a measurement of overt action at the moment of impression. Studies support that display and banner advertising create preference for brands if the advertisement is created correctly, even if the ad is only 'seen' at a subconscious level (i.e., the viewer has no conscious memory of having seen the ad).[6]

However, in the scientific and medical industries, the key measure of success often focuses on lead generation. At the very least, a click is some confirmation that an ad was seen by a living, breathing human being, so that we can continue to justify our advertising budgets. If the industry only values action as an effective measure of advertising, then we also need to contend with the level of natural noise within the internet so as to have realistic expectations.

What is the signal-to-noise ratio of clicks on the internet?

---

[5] D. Chaffey. "Display Advertising Clickthrough Rates." Smart Insights. Accessed online on March 22, 2016, at www.smartinsights.com/internet-advertising/internet-advertising-analytics/display-advertising-clickthrough-rates/.

[6] P. Chatterjee. "Are Unclicked Ads Wasted? Enduring Effects of Banner and Pop-Up Ad Exposures on Brand Memory and Attitudes." *Journal of Electronic Commerce Research*, Volume 9, No. 1, 2008. Accessed online on November 3, 2015, at web.csulb.edu/journals/jecr/issues/20081/Paper4.pdf.

In 2012, *Advertising Age* published a study by Ted McConnell that tested the potential effectiveness of banner advertising by discerning how much noise existed in the online advertising world.[7] In this case, 'noise' refers to meaningless data and clicks from robots. McConnell hypothesized that since the online world is a natural system—and every natural system contains noise—then the internet contained noise, too. The question was, how much?

To test his hypothesis, he created completely blank banner ads and purchased remnant ad space. He submitted the ads with a trackable link. The destination page asked clickers if they clicked on the link due to error or curiosity. The campaign received an average 0.08% CTR, so we see that the 0.1% I referenced earlier is close to the natural noise of the internet. This simple and brilliant test reveals how many people click on banner ads for reasons other than interest in the product or message. In this test, half of the clickers indicated the click was a mistake, and the other half indicated they clicked due to curiosity. Robots, accidental clicks, and systems that index the internet also contribute to this noise.

In relatively small, captive industries such as science and medicine, where the relationship between digital traffic and commerce is not dictated by volume but rather through deep interactions, the signal-to-noise ratio of online display advertising supports the notion that scientists and healthcare practitioners are not engaging with this traditional form of media communications.

Scientists Are Increasingly Engaging on Social Media

Although scientists have a propensity for privacy and are opting out of engagement on traditional media with companies, they are adopting social media channels as their central communications modalities to connect with their entire sphere of family, friends, peers and even brands.[8]

---

[7]T. McConnell. "How Blank Display Ads Managed to Tot Up Some Impressive Numbers." *Advertising Age*, July 23, 2012. Accessed online on November 3, 2015, at adage.com/article/digital/incredible-click-rate/236233/.

[8]R. Richard Van Noorden. "Online collaboration: Scientists and the social network." *Nature*, August 13, 2014. Accessed online on November 8, 2015, at www.nature.com/news/online-collaboration-scientists-and-the-social-network-1.15711.

When *Persuading Scientists* was first published in 2012, our industry still contended with validating whether social media would become a viable component of scholarly and business communications. The landscape has changed dramatically since then, and to synthesize the future of communications, we need to consider the following trends:

- Today, social media sites such as Facebook supply us with our entertainment and news and have completely changed how we connect with people, replacing the handwritten letter, postcard, email, telephone, video call, address book and television. Over a billion people engage on Facebook alone on a daily basis.[9]
- Microblogging platforms such as Twitter are instantaneous forms of news and serve as a predictive indicator of which information will become more important. (There is a statistically-significant correlation between the number of times a new scholarly article is tweeted in the first three days after publication and the number of citations that the same article will eventually receive in other scholarly articles.)[10]
- Professional network systems such as LinkedIn are changing how we make and maintain business connections. LinkedIn alone contains over 410 million users[11] and provides the most sophisticated professional segmentation opportunities of any medium.
- Even science-specific social media platforms such as ResearchGate, with over 9 million registered users,[12] are rapidly becoming communities where vibrant sharing, discussion and collaboration takes place between scientists.

The world of communications is rapidly changing and becoming noisier. Content offerings have exploded in number with each vying for limited time and attention. Mere content production will continue to have diminishing returns.

---

[9]Facebook. "Company Info." Accessed online on March 22, 2016, at newsroom.fb.com/company-info/.
[10]G. Eysenbach. "Can Tweets Predict Citations? Metrics of Social Impact Based on Twitter and Correlation with Traditional Metrics of Scientific Impact." *Journal of Medical Internet Research*, Vol 13, No 4 (2011): Oct-Dec. Accessed online on November 8, 2015, at www.jmir.org/2011/4/e123/.
[11]LinkedIn. "About LinkedIn." Accessed online on March 22, 2016, at press.linkedin.com/about-linkedin.
[12]ResearchGate. Accessed online on March 22, 2016, at www.researchgate.com.

Marketers need to ensure any content they produce will be worth a scientist's attention, which is a difficult task for companies whose primary expertise revolves around traditional channels instead of social channels.

2. MOBILITY CHANGES HOW SCIENTISTS CONSUME CONTENT

In *The Mobile Commerce Revolution*,[13] authors Tim Hayden and Tom Webster point out that humans have been mobile for millions of years—and only in the most recent two centuries did we transition to sitting. We are mobile creatures, our brain chemistry is optimized for being upright, and it is no wonder that smartphones today serve as our most intimate connection to the world. You can easily take a historical tour of this world by searching for anything from the earliest known cave paintings (humanity's oldest 'content') all the way to a scientific discovery published this morning.

We keep our mobile devices nearby day and night, and they usually dictate our first and last thoughts and interactions every day. Chances are high that your own mobile device is within arm's reach at this very moment.

How is the concept of mobility changing the way scientists and clinicians consume content and make decisions? To answer this question, we must consider two critical effects of mobile technology:

1. The buying journey is no longer a linear, deductive process.
2. The disappearing keyboard fuels the need for narrative.

Let us dive into both of these critical factors and explore their significance in the future of marketing.

Goodbye, Tidy Marketing Funnel. Hello, Messy Customer Buying Journey.

Due to new forms of mobility, the traditional marketing and sales funnel is collapsing. With information available any time and anywhere, audiences

---

[13] T. Hayden, T. Webster. *The Mobile Commerce Revolution: Business Success in a Wireless World.* Indianapolis, IN: Que Publishing, 2015.

can stay disengaged, bouncing inside and outside of marketing content—and perhaps in and out of the company's domain and purview—and then dive right into the final stages of purchase.

In 2012, *Harvard Business Review* published a critical finding by Corporate Executive Board (CEB) authors claiming that prospective customers complete nearly 60% of a complex sales decision before ever making contact with a company.[14] That data point frightens many executives since it means audiences make decisions before the company can employ its usual tactics to engage in dialogue, deploy sales tactics or attempt to persuade them in other ways. Prospects have educated themselves by the time they express interest in a product or service. When this happens, the company-prospect conversation focuses on the transactional aspects of the sale, which degrades the company's ability to maximize the sale based on value.

The ubiquitous access to information through mobile technologies is partly responsible for this dynamic, and it is destroying the tidy 'funnel' that marketers and sales people have used in order to understand consumer behavior. In the article "Branding in the Digital Age: You're Spending Your Money in All the Wrong Places," marketing strategist David C. Edelman claims that "far from systematically narrowing their choices, today's consumers take a much more iterative and less reductive journey."[15] Digital availability of information has created a new, far more circuitous 'customer buying journey,' where prospects make a choice slowly, by constant exposure to information through an ever-increasing number of channels, and then swoop in and engage in the act of purchasing at seemingly random times.

As prospective scientific customers grow more accustomed to using mobile technologies in their work, their decision-making habits are quickly changing. We need to develop new strategies, new content and new digital infrastructure

---

[14] B. Adamson, M. Dixon, N. Toman. "The End of Solution Sales." *Harvard Business Review*, July-August 2012. Accessed online on November 11, 2015, at hbr.org/2012/07/the-end-of-solution-sales.

[15] D. C. Edelman. "Branding in the Digital Age: You're Spending Your Money in All the Wrong Places." *Harvard Business Review*, December 2010. Accessed online on November 11, 2015, at hbr.org/2010/12/branding-in-the-digital-age-youre-spending-your-money-in-all-the-wrong-places.

to serve this increasingly complicated and elusive customer on their terms. Soon, the command-and-control sales tactics of yesterday will no longer apply.

Goodbye, QWERTY Keyboards. Hello 🎤

Increased mobility will obsolete the keyboard in the near future. Today, we are largely limited to communicating with our devices through keyboards and, as a result, through written text. Text will not form the internet's foundation for much longer. Instead, rich media will encompass most content with video, spoken word and interactive experiences.

We are starting to live in a world in which we regularly speak to our devices—and they speak back. Google's search engine and Apple's iPhone encourage us to speak to them so that they can improve the accuracy of their semantic understanding of regular spoken search phrases. Google's Android mobile OS and Apple's iOS come with speech-to-text software, so you can use your voice to search the internet or 'write' a text message.

None of the search modalities have human speech completely figured out—yet. Both Google and Siri need improvement. However, they *are* improving. As a result, Google and Siri award higher rankings to multimedia content such as video. Today, top search engine results often include such rich media as images and videos, and social media sites such as Pinterest and YouTube provide additional ways to share interesting and relevant rich media content. In addition, Google now provides higher rankings to mobile-friendly website designs—or responsive web design.[16] As content developers, we must contend with this ever-changing landscape at a time when most of our existing content is locked up in an antiquated text format—the PDF.

PDF technology is neither mobile-friendly, nor dynamic. Today, a large portion of content from science and healthcare companies is text-based and routinely shared via PDF. Publishers are rapidly evolving the housing and display of

---

[16]"Now is the Time for Responsive Design." *Forbes*, March 26, 2015. Accessed online on March 23, 2016, at www.forbes.com/sites/thesba/2015/03/26/now-is-the-time-for-responsive-design/.

scholarly articles for screen consumption. Some are merely mimicking the experience of the physical 'paper' while others are providing interactivity and videos. But many science companies lag behind, still producing traditional application notes that resemble the scientific paper and distributing them as PDF files, which further locks their content in this static, written format.

3. SCIENTISTS ARE INCREASINGLY SKEPTICAL OF BIG BUSINESS

In our surveys of the science and medical industries, we have sensed a change in the sentiments of scientists—especially those in research capacities—towards corporate entities since the Great Recession of the late 2000s.

Funding cuts during that recession hurt scientists and their work, whether they were in the public or private sector. If their funding was not directly affected, many knew someone who experienced cuts and had to abandon or significantly slow down progress on their research. Many scientists blame governments and 'big business' for their poor practices that led to the global economic meltdown in 2008. Though the Great Recession technically lasted for 18 months, ending in mid-2009,[17] the trajectory of research funding continues to lag the pre-recession trend as seen in Figure 01.03 (page 20).

Even scientists who work in private industry say that the Great Recession affected them negatively, and irrespective of their own employer's size, many scientists still carry this sentiment of distrust and skepticism about big business. While such skepticism does not enter into their daily work, scientists may be triggered and reminded of their sentiments when they see the multitudes of mergers and acquisitions taking place in our industry, as well as big business marketing tactics, shiny value propositions and slick corporate communications, along with overly-groomed PR strategies. One has to wonder to what extent they desire alternatives to the large corporation.

---

[17]"Great Recession." Wikipedia. Accessed online on November 24, 2015, at en.wikipedia.org/wiki/Great_Recession.

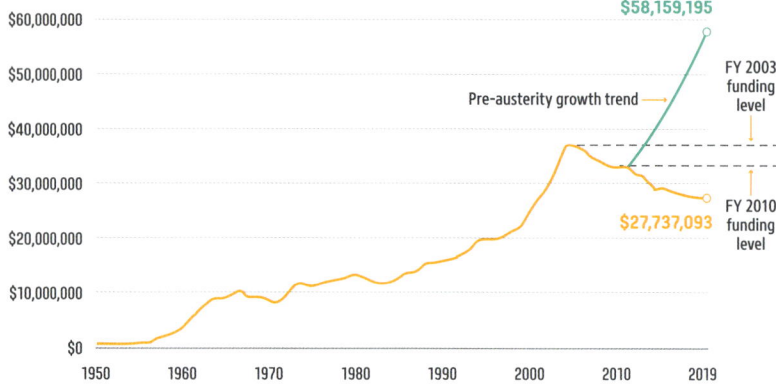

FIGURE 01.03 The United States National Institutes of Health, which is the world's largest funder of biomedical research, cut its funding during the Great Recession, changing the overall trajectory of science funding in the US.[18]

This is not to say that large corporations are at a disadvantage, but rather they do need to explore opportunities to engage such audiences as well as younger audiences who have been raised as digital natives. Companies need to humanize their communications in order to connect authentically with their audiences. Scientists and clinicians crave authenticity in the companies with which they engage. Assessing a vendor's values has become just as important as assessing their scientific instrument's price and specifications.

Where do scientists find such authenticity? Where and how can companies connect with scientists on a human-to-human level? Once again, the answer points to social media channels such as Facebook, which blurs the lines between personal and business relationships in every industry, including many business-to-business sectors. This dynamic can be to the benefit of both the company and the scientist. Many brands actively leverage social media channels to deliver a humanized experience. You have undoubtedly engaged with advertisements that tell a story. Sometimes these videos are three minutes in length, and yet you have

[18] Boadi. "Erosion of Funding for the National Institutes of Health Threatens U.S. Leadership in Biomedical Research." Center for American Progress, March 25, 2014. Accessed online on November 25, 2015, at www.americanprogress.org/issues/economy/report/2014/03/25/86369/erosion-of-funding-for-the-national-institutes-of-health-threatens-u-s-leadership-in-biomedical-research/.

willingly watched a three-minute commercial because it interested you. And unbeknownst to you, you have experienced the brand behind the commercial on a human level.

When scientists engage in an experience that delivers a humanized brand, they build a relationship that runs deeper than a more formal and stiff vendor-purchaser relationship. They gain a sense of the brand's authenticity and personality. In this way, a brand can become their friend. Instead of only being sold to, they are given an experience that communicates far more effectively than words.

THE NEW DIGITAL ERA IN SCIENCE AND HEALTHCARE

Clearly, marketing needs to evolve its processes and practices in order to form a new kind of meaningful relationship with scientists and clinicians. Traditional advertising content will continue to become ineffective. Relying on email programs in hopes of gaining a bump in the sales funnel will be seen as intrusive and will reflect poorly on the company's brand. Marketing needs to evolve in order to thrive in this new digital era.

For science and healthcare marketers, the opportunity here is far greater than merely adapting to the changing digital landscape. As products mature and companies find themselves in greater competition with parity product portfolios, they will realize that applying innovation to marketing presents tremendous untapped potential for winning.

The new digital era coincides with the age of marketing excellence in science and healthcare.

CHAPTER 2

The Digital Evolution of Marketing Science and Healthcare

A Guide to Developing Effective Marketing in the New Digital Era

SYNOPSIS

Communications technologies have changed the way scientists and clinicians consume content and make decisions, necessitating a new type of marketing practice for companies who want to stay ahead of the curve. The question is no longer whether companies need to adopt these new modalities, but rather how.

Thriving in the new digital era has little to do with technology but rather much more to do with how marketers can effectively create and execute a transition plan between today's traditional marketing and tomorrow's digital marketing practices. An effective transition plan needs a vision for the destination and steadily builds new capabilities, new processes and forms new habits across your organization. In the prior chapter, I provided a synthesis of the trends that you can use to build your vision. The next step is to map where we are today as an industry, so that we can chart a smart path toward a digital future that defies the transient popularity of specific tools, putting you and your organization on the right path for long-term success.

Specifically, I will discuss the following:

- A map of the traditional marketing funnel encompassing all of the industry's current activities
- The three major digital shifts in the landscape

- How to realistically evolve in the midst of the science and healthcare communications landscape

Understanding the key factors for successful implementation of a digital strategy will enable you to get ahead of the rapid pace of technology changes and drive toward your vision to create a strong marketing practice.

THE DIGITAL MATURITY OF SCIENCE AND HEALTHCARE

The concept of *digital* marketing is already redundant. All marketing is digital. Nearly all science and healthcare marketing contains major digital infrastructure and components. Marketers now even situate their age-old trade show activities within a larger digital strategy.

Strengthening your digital marketing capabilities is about much more than adapting to change. Most relevant indicators seem to show strong positive correlations between a company's digital sophistication and better financial performance.[19] Combined with the massive shift in their customers' sophistication, the vast majority of science and healthcare companies tread a path of constant development and implementation of digital strategies, trying to keep up with the constantly-shifting sands of the communications landscape. Larger companies take a top-down, technology-centric approach, while smaller companies typically employ a bottom-up, campaign-centric approach to going digital.

Few companies, however, are investing in the key factors that will ensure long-term digital success. Change is hard. Many marketers tell me that they feel stuck between their companies' corporate Information Technology infrastructure and policies that move too slowly to keep up with the pace of change or the massive amount of effort that their legacy marketing practices still consume, which keeps them tethered in yesterday's modalities.

---

[19] G. Westerman, D. Bonnet, A. McAfee. "The Advantages of Digital Maturity." *MIT Sloan Review*, November 20, 2012. Accessed online on March 8, 2016, at sloanreview.mit.edu/article/the-advantages-of-digital-maturity/.

For companies to effectively implement a successful digital strategy, we need to consider how to evolve by slowly divesting from legacy marketing activities in a methodical way, while gaining new capabilities, processes and habits. We also need to be guided by a strategy that keeps us as technology-neutral as possible, so as to ensure the longevity of our strategy.

To begin, we need to understand where we have been and to take inventory of the traditional content vehicles that we have and continue to expend energy toward in most science and healthcare marketing organizations.

THE TRADITIONAL MARKETING FUNNEL

Virtually all of the activities in which science and healthcare companies engage fit within the flow of the traditional marketing funnel, as illustrated in Figure 02.01. Let us walk through each stage of the funnel and map all of the activities that most marketers employ across each of the five stages of the traditional marketing funnel.

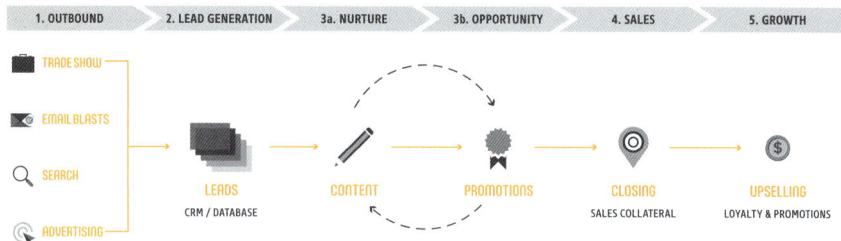

FIGURE 02.01 The traditional marketing funnel relies on lead generation and ongoing promotional contacts to identify opportunities to send to the sales pipeline.

1. **OUTBOUND**—Most companies engage in a series of outbound activities such as exhibiting at relevant trade shows, advertising, PR and direct mail/email communications in order to expose their messages to the largest number of target audiences that they can afford. Outbound communications have traditionally been expensive—commanding nearly 70% of marketing budgets in the industry, approximately a third of which goes to trade shows

alone[20]—but light on human resources needed for content development. From a resource perspective, the limiting factor for most companies is typically financial rather than talent.

2. **LEAD GENERATION**—In science and healthcare industries, lead generation often matters most. Other than at trade shows, where people make direct inquiries, leads are typically gathered as a result of a call-to-action on the company's website or on a discrete landing page, in exchange for something. Typically, lead generation requires the development of a piece of content or give-away to signal an equitable value exchange for the prospect, who uses their contact details as currency to 'buy' the free offer. While this makes logical sense, it also signals that the relationship with the company is nothing more than a transactional exchange.

3. **NURTURE & OPPORTUNITY**—Companies typically segment generated leads and add them to the email program, where marketers craft routine, ongoing content in order to develop and identify those who are interested or 'sales-ready.' Typically, the company creates newsletter or product-related content. These content channels usually cost little but take more internal resources to produce. When asked, an overwhelming number of science and healthcare marketers claim that the nurture and opportunity parts of the funnel are the most strategically critical to the overall success of their program, as they enable the company to build a lasting relationship with those expensive leads that have been generated through time. Unfortunately, these efforts prove largely ineffective, increasing market noise, annoying recipients and slowly eroding the company's reputation.

4. **SALES**—If a lead expresses interest at any point in the funnel, they are ushered to the appropriate channels for the sales process to begin. Most companies consider this point the handoff from marketing to sales, but marketing's job continues through the sales process. For the sales team

---

[20]H. Ghanadan. "Current Dynamics in Marketing Science: Results of the 2012 Survey of Science Marketers." *Linus Report*, September 2012. Data available at www.thelinusgroup.com/CatalyticExperiences/Supplements.

to succeed, marketing needs to arm them with appropriate collateral and materials to win the sale. The constant production of sales material has been the cornerstone of content development in the vast majority of companies' marketing departments and has been, in part, the main ball-and-chain preventing a more rapid digital evolution. While few companies print sales collateral these days, a vast majority use PDFs to create and distribute such material. As mentioned, the PDF format is the closest digital version of a static paper brochure, taking precious resources away from developing engaging experiences.

5. **GROWTH**—Sales and marketing split the role of growing the share-of-wallet from an existing customer base with loyalty incentives, to upsell or cross-sell relevant products. This powerful aspect of marketing holds tremendous potential for many companies. Success requires the company to have a current and detailed database with an in-depth profile of each customer, purchase history and a record of interactions with the company. Few companies have this level of detail today.

Most marketing departments expend all of their financial and human resources on activities across this funnel. Preparing for evolution requires auditing the resources expended in these activities. This informative and empowering exercise educates marketers as to how much content they are already producing.

In the prior chapter, we determined the massive shifts in the communications landscape through the lens of audiences and technology. In order to prepare for our marketing evolution, we need to be specific as to how these changes map to the traditional marketing funnel.

THE THREE MAJOR SHIFTS WITHIN THE MARKETING FUNNEL

These central questions drive the basis of a digital strategy.

- Where do social media and marketing automation technologies fit into the traditional marketing funnel?

- What role should the company's own website play in the vast proliferation of digital properties that house and disseminate content?
- How much credence should marketers give to search engines?

But the most important question in crafting a transition plan is: Where do these technologies fit within the current activities of the marketing department? Let us graph the full utility of these technologies into the traditional funnel, so that we can create a methodical approach to orchestrating the necessary change. Figure 02.02 provides this map.

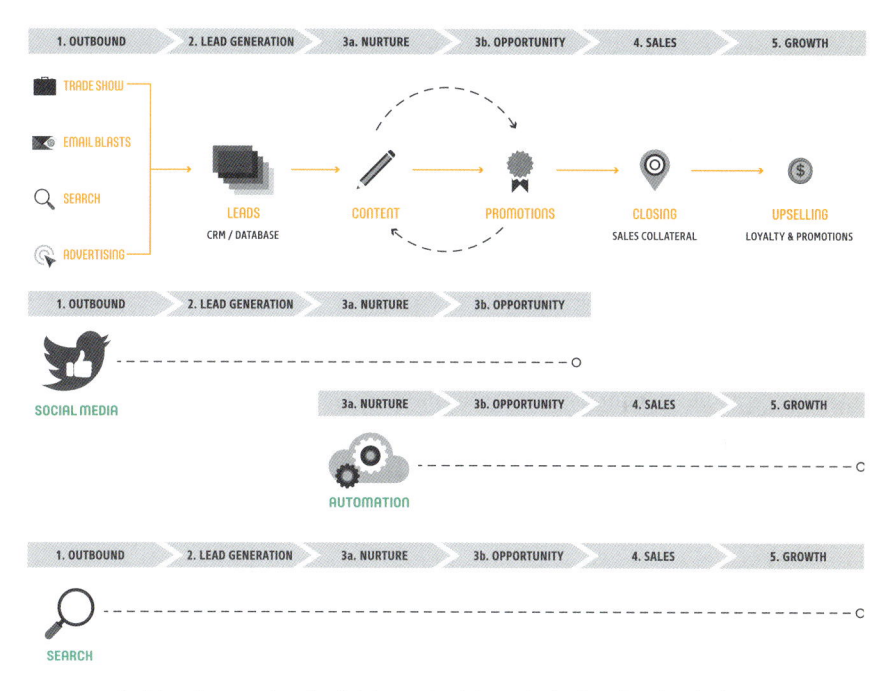

FIGURE 02.02 Social media can replace the first four parts of the marketing funnel, and marketing automation technologies can cover the last four sections of the funnel.

Where Social Media Fits

Many science and healthcare marketers have long ignored social media, justifying that no scientist or clinician will venture onto sites such as Facebook when looking for a product for the lab or clinic. While this is a logical statement, it is also short-sighted. While scientists do not spend their time on social media to search for products, they still spend time on social media. And this time is redirected from time spent on traditional media channels—and even in their own email inbox. While they do not actively seek products on such sites, social media represents one of the few and growing channels through which marketers can reach their audiences.

Social media has permanently changed the way we communicate on every level, necessitating that companies communicate differently than before. This holds true in complex business-to-business industries such as science and many healthcare markets. As discussed in the previous chapter, both the technology and audiences' own propensities are shifting their predispositions toward social relevance of content. Marketers have known this for some time. As early as 2011, most marketers in science and healthcare technology companies believed that social media would play a major role in their future marketing mix.[21] They just did not know how to employ it. As of late 2015, many companies still do not know exactly where social media should fit within their overall marketing funnel or how to evolve toward this social future.[22]

While several powerful science-focused social media platforms have gained mainstream adoption, it is critical to discuss the mainstream social platforms that dominate society's communications such as Facebook, Twitter and LinkedIn.

As Figure 02.02 illustrates, such social media platforms can replace all of the infrastructure needed to move through the first four steps of the traditional marketing funnel. Marketers can create specific pages and leverage the advertising options that these platforms offer for *outbound*, gain followers to the page, which is equally as valuable as traditional *lead generation*, then regularly publish content to *nurture* the audience and pepper the content with strong calls-to-action to generate *opportunities*. All of these steps can be easily managed on the

---

[21]H. Ghanadan. "Where Life Science Marketing is Headed: Results from the 2011 Quantitative Study of the Dynamics of Science Marketing." *Linus Report*, July 18, 2011. www.thelinusgroup.com/CatalyticExperiences/Supplements.
[22]Results from The Linus Group's 2015 survey of science and healthcare marketers, published to controlled audiences only. Data available at www.thelinusgroup.com/CatalyticExperiences/Supplements.

social media platforms themselves, offering a few key benefits over the traditional marketing channels:

1. **MORE AUDIENCE TARGETING OPTIONS**—Social media sites are not just for kids, and the lines between business and personal communications are being blurred. Scientists of all ages are on Facebook, Twitter and LinkedIn, and they engage with content that interests them. These sites offer excellent targeting opportunities through sophisticated algorithms and the ability to target further based on demographics and content habits.

2. **MORE AFFORDABLE**—Both through the sites' own advertising as well as through audience aggregators, reaching target audiences is less expensive than many other traditional media.

3. **MORE MAGNIFIED**—Instead of the traditional marketing funnel, which is linear and narrows as it progresses toward sales, any piece of content published on social media that is intended for any part of the funnel has the chance to spread. Like anyone, scientists and clinicians are inspired to share the content that they deem as representing their own views or their personalities, resulting in potential magnification of content.

4. **MORE EFFICIENT**—The infrastructure of building a page, publishing updates, uploading and hosting videos and providing calls-to-action are all built into the social media sites' functionality, making it far less technologically challenging to deploy a digital marketing campaign.

As most marketers know, the key to social media success is not the technology or the budgets, but rather it is about internal resources and the right kind of content. To evolve, marketers can slowly plan a transition that frees up time and traditional marketing budgets from traditional marketing modalities and applies them toward social media.

Where Marketing Automation Fits

Marketing automation software enables marketers to serve specific content to individual audiences based on their demographics and behavior. This type of software creates profiles for every audience member and installs a small tracking code on the user's computer (called a cookie), which then allows long-term tracking of the individual's behavior on the company's website and through email communications. This makes logical sense for marketers and presumes that audiences would be delighted to receive information that is highly targeted and pertinent to them.

Marketing automation becomes useful in ushering captured leads through the decision journey toward a sale. It can help grow a company's share-of-wallet, enhancing the latter four stages of the traditional marketing funnel. If implemented well, such software can provide tremendous value and benefits, including:

1. **MORE TARGETING OPTIONS**—No one wants to receive irrelevant messages. Marketing automation software allows marketers to develop targeted schemas based on specific profiles and behaviors (i.e., if an individual has clicked on one type of content in the past).

2. **MORE FEEDBACK**—With these schemas, marketers can identify each prospect's exact location along the decision-making journey based on behaviors.

3. **LONGER-LASTING CAMPAIGNS**—With the ability to develop multi-touch campaigns based on the audience's behavior, marketers can create longer-lasting 'dialogs' with audiences, based on each individual's own timeline. Every behavior, whether an action or lack of action, can trigger an automated next step through this software.

4. **MORE VERSATILITY**—Marketing automation tools can guide users to prep their site in advance of an instrument delivery, provide automated training or post-sale support and provide invaluable tracking data to companies about each individual customer.

5. **MORE CAPABILITIES**—Many software packages enable easy design of landing pages and forms, lowering the technology barrier to generating digital campaigns.

Marketing automation software is an excellent class of tools for marketers in any size company, as it democratizes the ability to develop sophisticated digital campaigns. However, it does present two major drawbacks that few science and healthcare companies are able to handle.

First, marketing automation's effectiveness depends upon the fidelity and hygiene of the company's database of customers and prospects. Since the power of marketing automation lies in the ability to develop targeted campaigns, marketers need to have enough data about their audiences to create targeted content. Unfortunately, most companies' databases are suboptimal to fully leverage the power of marketing automation. Our surveys show—and experience confirms it—that 66% of companies in science and healthcare have multiple databases, cannot identify their customers from their prospects or have no way to easily target based on specialty, application or industry. Absent a well-segmented database, marketing automation will not provide the benefits outlined earlier.

Second, the underlying technology framework for marketing automation programs rests on cookies and email and on the premise that audiences want targeted information. In as early as 2010, only 20% of Americans expressed an interest in targeted advertising in a survey, whereas 64% felt that targeting invaded their privacy.[23] Even though people typically choose convenience over privacy,[24] the fact that they find targeting distasteful means overuse of marketing automation technology could significantly erode a company's brand perceptions.

With these caveats, marketers will still greatly benefit from installing marketing automation platforms if they use the technology responsibly and with the intention of providing genuine value to audiences with each touch, rather than bombarding the industry with promotional material. Used well, marketing automation can enable marketers to nurture their audiences and ripen opportunities before seeing those opportunities through to sales and growth.

---

[23]A. M. McDonald, L. F. Cranor. "Americans' attitudes about internet behavioral advertising practices," WPES '10 *Proceedings of the 9th annual ACM workshop on Privacy in the electronic society*, pgs 63-72. Assoc. for Computing Machinery, New York, NY, 2010. Accessed online on March 10, 2016, at dl.acm.org/citation.cfm?id=1866929.

[24]RJ. Davidson. "You Say You'd Give Up Online Convenience for Privacy—But You're Lying." *Money*, June 25, 2014. Accessed online on March 10, 2016, at time.com/money/2902134/you-say-youd-give-up-online-convenience-for-privacy-but-youre-lying/.

Where Search Engines Fit

Search engines offer an opportunity to drive relevant audiences to a company's offerings. At its most basic form, a relevant click-through from a search page should be the most valuable type of traffic any company receives. After all, the interaction occurs at the very moment that the prospect demonstrates interest. Since audiences engage with companies at every stage in their cycle, visibility on search engines can positively affect every stage of the traditional marketing funnel.

This is not news to marketers in the science and healthcare industries, as they have increased their search advertising steadily over the past decade and constantly try to gain visibility in organic search results.

But search engines represent a much larger and more critical opportunity for marketers.

As consumer sentiments change and email and direct communications become outmoded or despised, scientists and clinicians will increase their distance from companies. Then, search engine visibility will become central to a marketing organization's success. After consumer sentiment changes, emailing and tracking individuals become illegal and audiences opt out of the more traditional channels, search will become one of the few doors remaining open for marketers to connect with audiences—and it will be fully on the audience's terms. Essentially, our audiences will say, "if you are that important to me and my work, you will show up when I need you."

Succumbing to the above statement relinquishes marketing's role and allows our audience to define us. Limiting your search engine strategy to merely building equity of the company's offerings, however, foregoes an opportunity to shape the decision-journey of the audience earlier on, before audiences even realize that they need you. Instead of imagining your audience looking for your product, imagine what they may be searching for prior to recognizing they need your products. Capture their attention before they realize they need you, and you will shape their decision, rather than becoming a mere contestant in their choice.

Building equity on search engines takes time. As I discussed, search engines place higher precedence on content that is rich, interactive, popular and optimized for mobile devices. Creating this type of content is imperative and not trivial. But nothing worthwhile is trivial.

HOW TO APPROACH YOUR DIGITAL EVOLUTION

I am not a technology fetishist. I firmly believe that technology should serve strategies, instead of driving them. From this point of view, the only shift in marketing over the past 40 years is the rate of change itself. Even though new technologies are enabling novel types of communications, the major factors that affect companies' priorities have been going back and forth like a pendulum.

For example, the concept of branding waned in the early 2000s in favor of direct communications, only to come back to central importance now, once direct communications fail to deliver on their promise. It is called something different, but the goal is the same as it was in the 1990s when companies tried to gain awareness and signal desired behavior through brands. However, by the time the pendulum was able to swing all the way through its cycle and back, the world changed. Companies have new opportunities to brand themselves through new channels that did not exist the last time branding was in favor.

To chase a rapidly-shifting technology landscape is a recipe for perpetual reactivity. Instead, companies should build long-term, proactive strategies that ask how the changing trends of technology will work for them to realize their own vision.

In my synthesis, the three major shifts replacing traditional tactics within the marketing funnel are not mutually exclusive. They require a content strategy, a different class of content and the orchestration of experiences.

Three critical factors exist for any company's marketing today. They are central to the success of the company's brand in the digital landscape:

> **THOUGHT LEADERSHIP**—A bold stance about the customer's own future, causing thought-provoking discussions that will build true brand equity and draw real pull in the customer-empowered world where audiences keep companies at a distance until they have made the majority of their purchase decisions.
>
> **CATALYTIC EXPERIENCES**—Content that demonstrates the true value of a product, service or idea, engaging the entire human experience, delivered through stories rather than claims, explanations or written text. Such experiences provide the opportunity to leverage rich media to create interactive digital content that can be proliferated and shared through social channels and search engines. It also enables marketers to leverage the most proven technology for delivering meaningful messages to audiences that align with the evolution of the human brain's capability to fully understand information: stories.
>
> **HUMANIZATION**—An honest display of personification of companies, technologies or products as more than abstractions, but as humans interacting with scientists and healthcare providers as fellow humans.

These three interconnected facets of a marketing strategy work closely together and form the foundation for successful Content-Centric Marketing for Science and Healthcare.

Thought Leadership

Taking a proactive stance in the marketplace through thought leadership will enable marketers to gain widespread awareness, inspire debate and create pull by telling customers what they ought to care about. Ultimately, a strong thought leadership initiative generates actionable, measurable brand equity on search and social channels. Thought leadership is digital currency, and is a necessary part of a company's digital evolution. Without it, your content marketing will lack the vector to move your market from the state of understanding to the desired state of predisposition to, lastly, accepting your value proposition.

A strong thought leadership campaign can effectively replace the majority of the product-centric outbound and at least some technology-centric educational material, saving both human and budgetary resources while tremendously increasing the potency of the marketing organization.

Catalytic Experiences

Scientists or clinicians engage with traditional marketing less and less these days. Expected advertising headlines that tout the benefits of a product do not move audiences. Marketing needs to surprise, delight and move audiences to feel something. Moving an audience to feel something happens through an interactive and emotional experience—a Catalytic Experience—an un-ignorable illustration of a core common truth between the company and its audiences.

A Catalytic Experience tells the market a story, and it serves as the marquee experience of a campaign. Such stories are often driven through rich or immersive media such as video, photographs, info-graphics, virtual reality environments or interactive experiences and games—the same tactics that will continue to be more valuable to search engine algorithms as the world evolves from Boolean search toward natural language search in spoken word. Catalytic Experiences involve the types of content often shared on social media channels, as they not only resonate with scientists and clinicians on a personal, emotional level, they often help these audiences express what they think and how they feel to their own networks through sharing of the content.

Most marketing efforts lack a Catalytic Experience, and instead rely on quantity of content to entice audiences. Because of the content overload that already exists in science and healthcare, the efficacy of quantity-based content marketing will continue to diminish, while there is no shortage of attention that is given to an interactive experience that captures hearts and minds.

Humanization

People want to engage with people. Social engagement is predicated upon this universal human behavior. When we develop content, we need to consider social media as a highly effective channel for reaching an attention-challenged but connection-starved audience. When humanized content appears in newsfeeds in the form of stories, scientists consume it if it is relevant—especially in a world that blurs the lines between brands and 'brands as friends.'

As you consider developing content to support your social media channels, you need to take your brand's tone and voice into consideration. Rigid, corporate stances or obscure 'marketing speak' do not engage audiences. Whether through the use of a spokesperson, a social beacon, a meme or merely through an extensive development of a human tone and texture, you need to create a brand that is fluid, organic and breaks the cold, rigid corporate orthodoxies to embrace the warmth and organic nature of a humanized brand.

THE MODEL TO FOLLOW

Most lasting and effective digital evolution within science and healthcare companies will occur organically, through the silos of product marketers who want to maximize the power of the digital landscape to launch their product, increase their sales or fight their competitors. As a result of these efforts, they will gain new skills, build new habits and create best practices among their organizations, which will eventually require companies to contend with a top-down approach to orchestrate their digital evolution.

The foundation of a successful digital marketing program requires marketers to shape their audience's thinking through thought leadership, demonstrate their value through Catalytic Experiences and connect with their audience as human peers.

But it is not haphazard trial and error or idle emotional storytelling that will result in success. To succeed, you need a guide: a map for finding the right thought leadership stance, to tell your story in the right sequence, to strike the appropriate balance between logic and emotion and to evolve your brand. You need to adhere to a model to guide your decisions and develop the right strategy in the development of these critical aspects of digital marketing.

The model you choose should align with natural decision-making patterns of scientists and clinicians. In the following chapter, we will tour the Content-Centric Model for Marketing Science and Healthcare and situate it among three other popular models.

CHAPTER 3

The Model Model

Situating the Content-Centric Model Among Other Sales and Marketing Models

SYNOPSIS

Countless models for sales and marketing exist—documented in innumerable books, recorded as TED Talks or sold as part of proprietary systems. All claim they have the secret to success. Some are applied to specific industries while others claim to be universal. Most say the same thing, and few rise to the top.

So what is a marketer or sales executive to do in deciding to implement one or several models within a science or healthcare organization? This chapter reveals patterns and points of intersection between several of the most popular models in marketing and sales. In this chapter, I provide the necessary concepts for you to evaluate how to discern the models that best fit your organization.

Specifically, I will discuss the following:

- A brief recap of the Content-Centric Model for Marketing Science and Healthcare, which I published in my first book, *Persuading Scientists*
- A comparison with Simon Sinek's 'Golden Circle' model
- A comparison with 'The Challenger Sale' model
- A contrast with the principles of the 'Inbound Marketing' model

Understanding these models can help close the sales-marketing divide and help unify teams.

THE CONTENT-CENTRIC MODEL FOR MARKETING SCIENCE AND HEALTHCARE

To achieve success in marketing a science or healthcare product, solution or brand, you need to display thought leadership, deliver your message through a Catalytic Experience and humanize your voice. Stories need to be told instead of claims made. Often, marketers struggle to know what type of story works best for scientific audiences, or how to tell it.

Effective stories that truly move scientists and clinicians tend to follow a specific narrative pattern intrinsic to how these audiences make decisions.

Overview of the Scientific Mind and the Decision Journey

Let us delve into a map of how the scientific mind reacts to information, and why creativity is the inception of the scientific—and decision-making—journey.

Studying science trains a person's mind to dynamically move between *curiosity* and *skepticism*. Curiosity indicates the state of mind that is open to information, allowing a person to see and make novel observations. Skepticism prevents the scientist from believing everything they see or hear until they prove it to themselves. Curiosity and skepticism form the foundation of the scientific method. Every human becomes curious, and every human becomes skeptical. Scientific training further hones the deductive reasoning of a person to dynamically move back and forth between these two states with greater deftness.

People who are scientists are not just logical beings, however. They are human. As such, they are driven by both *objectivity* (logic) and *subjectivity* (emotion). As depicted in Figure 03.01 (page 44), mapping these two aspects provides us with a simplified map of how scientists may react to information.

On the logical side of the graph in Figure 03.01, the Scientific Method is overt: curiosity drives scientists to make an observation, create a *hypothesis*, and then *validate* that hypothesis through evidence to satisfy their skepticism. On the emotional side, scientists have a burst of *creativity* if they are curious and then have an emotional reaction to their observation. Conversely, if scientists are

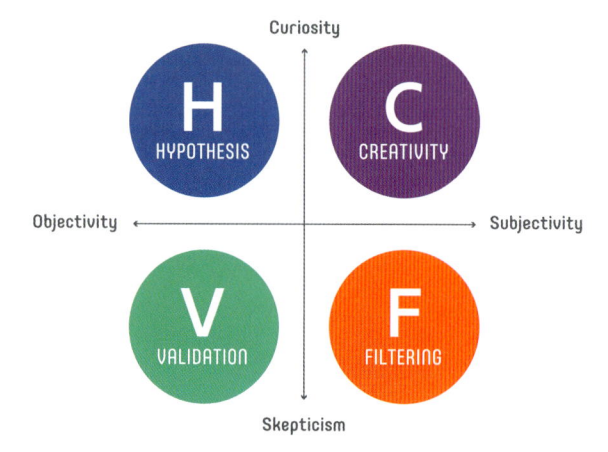

FIGURE 03.01 This simple framework is the underpinning of the Content-Centric Model for Marketing Science and Healthcare, and it distills down the Scientific Method, while adding to it the spectrum of emotion. The four quadrants that result from mapping these two states together give us an indication of how a scientist will react to stimulus, which in the form of marketing is content.

presented with information or observations that raise their skepticism and they have an emotional reaction against it, then they *filter* out that information.

Our understanding about the Scientific Method starts when the scientist makes an observation.[25] How do scientists decide which novel observation to follow and investigate? How do they decide the fields of study to which they will devote their careers? The Scientific Method only describes part of the full process. It is my belief that the scientific process actually begins when a scientist has a burst of creativity as a result of an emotional reaction to an insight, a realization, a result or an observation. This creativity is the driving force that motivates a scientist to endure daily failures in order to prove or disprove a hypothesis. In science and medical marketing, we tend to idealize the 'eureka moment' as the instant a breakthrough occurs at the end of a scientific experiment and process. Instead, the 'moment of creativity' happens earlier in the process and is far more emotionally resonant to a scientist. From creativity comes hypothesis and validation. Not surprisingly, the three phases of the scientist or clinician's decision journey follow these same states.

---

[25]"Scientific Method." Wikipedia. Accessed online on February 25, 2016, at en.wikipedia.org/wiki/Scientific_method.

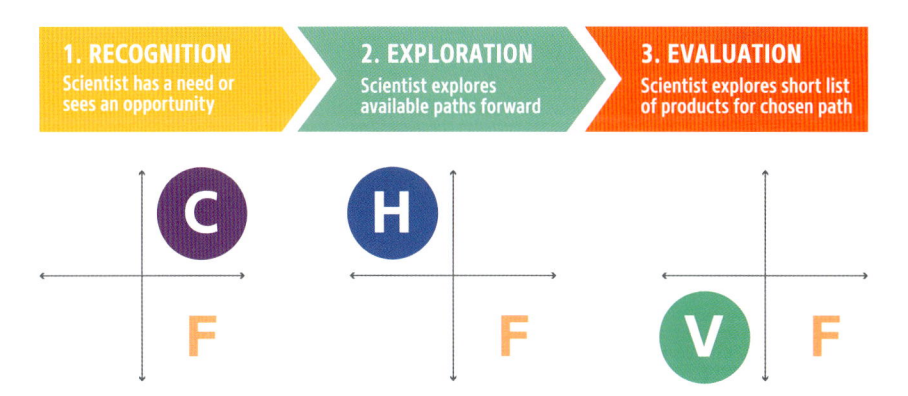

| 1. RECOGNITION | 2. EXPLORATION | 3. EVALUATION |
| Scientist has a need or sees an opportunity | Scientist explores available paths forward | Scientist explores short list of products for chosen path |

FIGURE 03.02 The three phases of the decision journey for scientists and clinicians mirror their path to discovery, and consists of a balance between their logic and emotions.

This decision-making path is applicable to more than scientists in a research environment. Applied scientists, engineers and clinicians follow this same path. The long-held standard of medical practice calls for 'differential diagnosis,' which teaches clinicians to make observations about their patient, and then methodically eliminate possibilities through data to validate their diagnosis. And yet, countless times, clinicians use their own intuition to navigate a patient to health.[26]

For scientists and clinicians to make a decision, they need to see an opportunity or recognize they have a need. This *recognition* typically results in a burst of creativity. During this process, they continue their work and may be unaware of a particular product need, but that creativity motivates them to *explore* the paths that are available to them in pursuit of making a hypothesis about the best way to satisfy their need. Only when they have formed a hypothesis do they *evaluate* the list of products and services that they have determined to be viable options for satisfying their need. This evaluation is in service of validation of their own hypothesis, and they evaluate the features, benefits and value propositions of the offering through the lens of their own hypothesis.

Traditional marketing and many models that claim to guide 'content marketing' practices are typically focused on persuasive tactics and raise skepticism in a

---

[26] J. Cole. *Trauma: My Life as an Emergency Surgeon*. New York: St. Martin's Press, 2011.

scientist or clinician too early in their decision journey. We must address this by awakening their curiosity first to have a burst of creativity, so they can lead themselves to their hypothesis. By the time they become skeptical, we need to be ready to validate their hypothesis. Scientists and clinicians need to feel that they are in the decision-making driver's seat. We need to engage with them using the right content at the right time. With activated creativity, scientists and clinicians become emotionally invested in the outcome. It is a subtle yet powerful change in how they experience their decision journey.

The Three Classes of Content

Earlier, I mentioned that stories need to be told in a particular order if we want them to land purposefully within the minds of our audiences. We do this by offering three classes of content, each of which are intended to reach the optimal psychological step within the appropriate points of our audience's decision journey.

Leadership content has one job—to make prospective customers curious so that they recognize they have a need.

Educational content, ideally, helps the scientist formulate the hypothesis about how they will meet their need. In this stage, we educate them about the need and provide them with the ingredients to develop their own hypothesis. Then we get out of the way and allow them to explore the different paths available to satisfy their need. In this stage, the scientist or clinician is in a logical mode and looking to form a hypothesis. Any sense of bias at this stage will drive them to skepticism and filtering.

Persuasive content forms the third content class. Once scientists formulate their hypothesis, they move into product evaluation. At this stage, they are looking to validate their own hypothesis. If we have done our job right, we have earned the right to persuade them and to share our value proposition.

RECOGNITION	EXPLORATION	EVALUATION
Scientists recognize they have a need or see an opportunity. The need may have always been there, but the moment of recognition brings the need into the scientist's consciousness.	Scientists explore all the paths that are available in satisfying their need or pursuing their opportunity. Extremely sensitive to bias at this stage, they look to formulate their own thinking.	Scientists review the short-list of commercial options that they have found to be relevant to them. For the first time, scientists are open to hearing value propositions about offerings and will chose the one that most closely validates their hypothesis.
Leadership Content	**Education Content**	**Persuasion Content**
Company asserts a point of view or provokes or challenges the audience about a topic that invokes curiosity, which enables them to recognize they have a need.	Company provides balanced, logical evidence to support its point of view, and invites scientists to make their own hypothesis about the issue at hand.	Company demonstrates the value proposition by providing validation to the hypothesis that they invited the scientist to consider.
CREATIVITY	HYPOTHESIS	VALIDATION

FIGURE 03.03 The above model describes three phases of a decision journey for a scientist, physician, engineer or others with scientific training. Note that the states of mind that need to be activated in order for the scientist to advance—creativity, hypothesis, validation—follow the same path as the scientific method. The three classes of content are designed to advance the scientist in their decision by satisfying these states of mind. Thus, communications efforts need to be tailored and optimized for reaching the desired state of mind and nothing more.

The Benefits of the Content-Centric Model for Marketing Science and Healthcare

Classical marketing practices are all based on the notion that awareness of a product leads to interest, followed by a desire for the product, ending in action on the part of the audience to purchase. In large part, the marketing mix within many companies is predicated on this Awareness, Interest, Desire and Action flow (AIDA).

When it comes to science and healthcare, the AIDA model is wrong.

In science and medical industries, awareness about a product is not enough to hook the audience to engage in their decision journey. Also, following the AIDA model leads marketers to building a passive marketing program, essentially only delivering persuasion content across the entire purchasing journey, which raises skepticism too early, leading to filtering the vast majority of the marketing efforts.

As I mentioned earlier, research has found that technical customers complete 60% of the decision journey before contacting the potential vendor. This means that audiences have already gone through their own moment of recognition and exploration to formulate their hypothesis about the best way to satisfy their need. By the time they make contact, they are looking to validate their hypothesis. Unless the vendor has played a role shaping that hypothesis, they are in a reactive position by the time the customer makes contact.

The Content-Centric Model provides the framework to deliver the most appropriate stories at the right time to influence the scientist or clinician's decision journey earlier. In this way, they receive messages about the product when they are in the right mindset to receive it—and do so without filtering but to satisfy their skepticism.

In my experience working with science and healthcare companies, I have found the Content-Centric Model to be the missing piece in marketing departments. Employing the model will bring two main benefits that will result in far more effective marketing:

1. It provides a more customer-centric rubric for managers to make decisions about producing the right kind of content to support the scientist's own decision journey, rather than contriving some funnel and forcing audiences through it.

2. It aligns all of the vehicles and tactics to play a specific role in advancing the scientist's decision journey forward, and aligns all of those vehicles within an over-arching architecture.

Aligning the Content-Centric Model with the Traditional Funnel

The three phases of the Content-Centric Model for Marketing Science and Healthcare align with the steps of the traditional marketing funnel, as depicted in Figure 03.04.

| OUTBOUND | LEAD GENERATION | NURTURE | OPPORTUNITY | SALES | GROWTH |

| LEADERSHIP | EDUCATION | PERSUASION |

FIGURE 03.04 The three phases of the Content-Centric Model for Science and Healthcare maps to the traditional marketing funnel, irrespective of the specific vehicles that are used. This provides the key to developing strategies that are independent of technologies and trends.

1. Leadership content combines targeted lead generation with a strong outbound message. In this model, the role of outbound channels becomes driving the audience to recognize they have a need and not about displaying a product or solutions.

2. Educational content provides an excellent way to nurture leads, predisposing them to the company's point of view and subtly ushering them to form a hypothesis about the best path for satisfying their need. Here, the company refers to its offerings only in calls-to-action to turn a lead into an opportunity.

3. Persuasion content takes center stage when the audience has taken advantage of the offer to learn more about the commercial offerings and has entered the sales framework, which will grow the customer over time.

The Content-Centric Model for Marketing Science and Healthcare provides you the ability to create a strong, lasting and consistent strategy and the confidence to apply this to whatever tools, technologies and trends you want to leverage. With this overlay between the traditional marketing funnel and the Model, you know how to orchestrate the right part of the story on social channels and how to appropriately use marketing automation and your own web properties.

While the Model is founded on how scientists and healthcare professionals make decisions, it greatly overlaps with several other marketing and sales models that have gained recent interest within the broader business community. Let us compare the Model to a popular model for branding—Simon Sinek's 'Golden

Circle'[27]—another marketing model—'InBound Marketing' methodology[28]—and the most provocative sales model in the last several decades—the Corporate Executive Board's (CEB) 'Challenger' model.[29]

WHY, WHY, WHY? THE CENTRAL QUESTION BEHIND 'THE GOLDEN CIRCLE'

In 2009, Simon Sinek delivered a talk at TEDxPuget Sound that spread like wildfire. His talk became the second-most-watched talk on TED.com, with 24 million views to date.[30] He later developed the idea into the book *Start With Why*. Marketers and even corporate executives love The Golden Circle because it is a deceptively simple model yet inspiring and universally applicable.

Sinek observed that people, companies and organizations that defy the norm in terms of accomplishments communicate, act and think differently than everyone else—and they communicate in the same pattern. Sinek codified this pattern 'The Golden Circle.' He states that almost all people know what they do, and some know how they do it, but very few know why they do it. As a result, most people talk about what they do, some people talk about how, yet few discuss why.

Sinek argues that the *why* forms the core of connections between people and inspires action. Most companies, however, talk about their *what* by referring to their technology, products and solutions. They discuss how solutions help customers achieve more, yet they rarely mention why they do the things they do. Sinek discovered that successful communicators "think, act and communicate from the inside out." They begin with *why*, then they move to *how* and then they talk about *what* as the final piece of their story.

---

[27] Simon Sinek. "How great leaders inspire action." TEDxPuget Sound. Accessed online on February 2, 2016, at www.ted.com/talks/simon_sinek_how_great_leaders_inspire_action?language=en.
[28] HubSpot. "The Inbound Methodology." Accessed online on February 2, 2016, at www.hubspot.com/inbound-marketing.
[29] M. Dixon, B. Adamson. *The Challenger Sale: Taking Control of the Customer Conversation*. New York: Penguin Publishing Group, 2011.
[30] Cloe Shasha. "How Simon Sinek's TEDx success made him think deeply about trust." TEDBlog, July 10, 2014. Accessed online on February 2, 2016, blog.ted.com/how-simon-sineks-tedx-fame-made-him-think-deeply-about-trust-issues/.

THE GOLDEN CIRCLE

Every single person knows WHAT they do → **WHAT**

Some people know HOW they do it → **HOW**

Very few people know WHY they do it → **WHY**

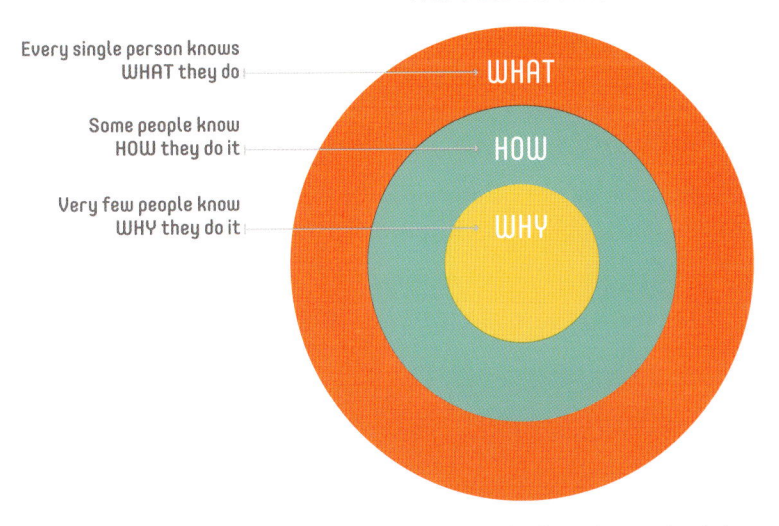

FIGURE 03.05 Simon Sinek's 'The Golden Circle' model claims that our 'why' is at the core of our being, and it is the information that inspires action because it is the emotional signal that cuts through the rational part of our brain and connects with our limbic brain that is responsible for decision-making.[31]

Sinek stresses the idea that "people don't buy what you do. They buy why you do it." The why resonates with our audience's limbic brain, which is the emotional part of the brain that controls behavior change. To succeed, it is important for companies to uncover their why and to attract people who believe what the company believes. According to Sinek, customers with the same beliefs make the best customers. Since potential customers take action for themselves—and not for a company—it is valuable to discover the core common truths that connect audience and company. The what occupies the neocortex, which is responsible for the dissemination of language yet has no decision-making ability. If we only talk about the what, all we do is feed the analytical part of the brain, the part that seeks understanding but does not generate action. This powerful discovery can become the basis for companies to articulate their brands authentically.

---

[31] S. Sinek. *Start With Why.* New York: Penguin Group, 2009.

Connecting The Golden Circle and the Content-Centric Model for Marketing Science and Healthcare

A clear and direct connection exists between these two models, yet the Content-Centric Model remains more applicable for science and healthcare. In the Content-Centric Model, Leadership content is the necessary piece to activate curiosity. This content asserts a provocative point of view in the marketplace while identifying the core common beliefs between company and audience. This Leadership content resonates emotionally with the audience to pique their curiosity so they can have that burst of creativity. Loosely described, this dynamic is akin to the *Why* in The Golden Circle.

1. RECOGNITION
LEADERSHIP
To activate curiosity, marketers need to assert a provocative point of view.

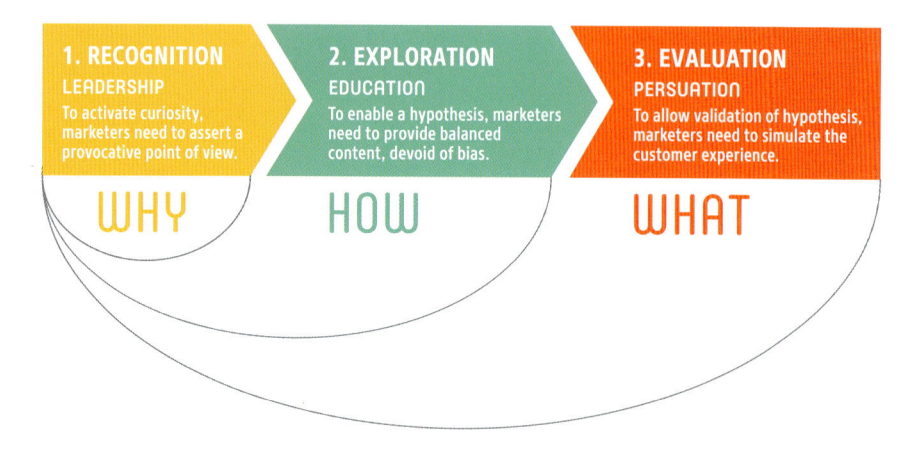

2. EXPLORATION
EDUCATION
To enable a hypothesis, marketers need to provide balanced content, devoid of bias.

3. EVALUATION
PERSUASION
To allow validation of hypothesis, marketers need to simulate the customer experience.

WHY   HOW   WHAT

FIGURE 03.06 Transposing the three phases of the Content-Centric Model over The Golden Circle, it is evident that the former is a specialized version of the more universally-applicable latter.

Respectively, the Education content is meant to answer the *How* and, finally, the Persuasion content describes the *What* in The Golden Circle. Due to this high degree of correlation between these two models, we sometimes articulate a brand's narrative through The Golden Circle as well, in order to evaluate the arc of the story through an intersecting point of view.

THE MIGHTY CHALLENGER

In 2001, Matthew Dickson and Brent Adamson, in *The Challenger Sale: Taking Control of the Customer Conversation* (2011), changed the definition of a good salesperson. Dickson and Adamson work at the Corporate Executive Board, which focuses on sales and marketing strategy for business-to-business markets. They researched and ranked the performance of salespeople in complex sales situations and conducted factor analysis after surveying thousands of salespeople and correlating their methodology and personalities to performance. Prior to their research, common wisdom among sales professionals heralded relationships as the most critical factor for sales success. According to Dickson and Adamson, however, only 7% of top sales performers are considered relationship builders.

Their research revealed five distinct traits that define different types of sales people, and the percentage of top sales performers who displayed each set of characteristics (in parentheses):

- **THE HARD WORKER** (17%)—Self-motivated salesperson who typically puts in extra effort.
- **THE PROBLEM SOLVER** (14%)—Detail-oriented salesperson who works to remove obstacles.
- **THE LONE WOLF** (25%)—Highly confident salesperson who only acts on her own instincts but may be hard to manage.
- **THE RELATIONSHIP BUILDER** (7%)—Friendly salesperson who spends time getting to know his customers and gets along with everyone.
- **THE CHALLENGER** (39%)—A highly knowledgeable salesperson with a unique point of view about the customer's business.

Surprisingly, the relationship builders accounted for the lowest percentage of top-performers in their research cohort, and the category labeled 'Challenger' accounted for more top-performers than any other group of behaviors in sales people. Dickson and Adamson discovered that the Challengers illuminate provocative elements of their customer's work. These qualities set Challengers apart from their peers, and they drive a repeatable pattern for how they take control of the sales conversation:

1. They challenge the status quo about the customer;
2. They educate the customer to believe their point of view; and
3. They create a tailored solution to fit the point of view.

This sales model became popular in 2011, and numerous science and medical technology companies have implemented it. In the model, the salesperson gains emotional connection, instills the necessary beliefs and takes positive action. The salesperson begins by challenging the status quo of the customer and reframes how the customer views an issue. During reframing, the Challenger shares an insight to evoke emotional resonance in the customer. The salesperson provides guided education to encourage the prospect to have their own insight that 'the world is different' and that the resulting need is credible. At this point, the salesperson reveals tailored solutions to satisfy the prospect's newly discovered need.

Assessing the Challenger Model

The Challenger Model reveals that personality traits have little to do with sales success, so companies hiring sales teams have more power to teach virtually anyone the necessary tools to become a top performer. With the Challenger Model, sales reps provide genuine value with every sales call because they aim to educate the customer. The resulting conversations turn into high-energy discussions for both sides at every stage of the process, and the sales rep gains the highest level of respect and credibility in the eyes of their customer.

The Challenger Model does pose a few difficulties for companies who choose to use it. The company must take a position in the world instead of being willing to sell anything to anyone. While in marketing strategy this is referred to as segmentation, I have noticed that some companies are not willing to make this level of commitment to focus. This necessary point of view forms the foundational material for the challenge. The company must invest in discovering the right challenges to define the customer's needs—and the need must be both real and big.

Another potential difficulty occurs when companies use incorrect challenges. If this happens, salespeople can rush into the market before realizing they are unprepared to fully resonate with their audience. Marketing and sales need to work closely together to prevent such situations. The Challenger Model requires a company to conduct the necessary research, find the challenges, develop and deliver the right content for the sales people and provide sales with 'air cover' by reframing the audience's mindset through its marketing tactics.

Connecting the Challenger Model and the Content-Centric Model for Marketing Science and Healthcare

Again, I see a high degree of correlation. The *challenge* is exactly the same as the Content-Centric Model's Leadership content, which provides a provocative point of view to encourage the prospect's recognition of a need. In both models, providing education is the necessary middle step to allow the customer to arrive at their own hypothesis about the provocation or need. The tailored solution of the Challenger Model is akin to Persuasion content.

I believe that applying the Content-Centric Model will prepare any scientific marketing department to proactively develop and deliver the fuel to empower sales people with the right narrative, irrespective of which sales models are being implemented.

THE ALLURE OF INBOUND

In 2009, Brian Halligan and Dharmesh Shah, cofounders of the HubSpot marketing automation software platform, wrote a book called *Inbound Marketing: Get Found Using Google, Social Media, and Blogs*, which was subsequently updated in 2014 with the revised subtitle *Attract, Engage and Delight Customers Online*[32] and popularized the concept through the successful *InBound* annual conference. The phrase 'inbound marketing' describes the continuation of the customer's journey through marketing channels once the customer ventures

---

[32]B. Halligan, D. Shah. *Inbound Marketing: Attract, Engage and Delight Customers Online*. Hoboken, NJ: John Wiley and Sons, 2014.

onto the company's exclusive channels (e.g., their company's website). In fact, inbound marketing is not a new phenomenon. It has long been used by experienced marketers to distinguish between outbound efforts such as advertising or direct mail.

Rather, the popularization of InBound as a nouveau concept (which I will distinguish from a normal part of the marketing mix by capitalizing the 'I' and 'B' in the word) signifies the sentiment that in today's digital world, developing a strong inbound channel will naturally draw visitors, requiring less overt 'outbound' effort that has traditionally been too expensive while demonstrating decreasing efficacy.

The balance between pushing messages (outbound) and pulling audiences (inbound) is still a delicate art and depends on the objectives of the marketer. Inbound marketing programs still use outbound activities yet keep inbound methods as the strategic center of the marketing mix. The inbound channel is increasingly more powerful—and good content can attract, engage and delight customers.

Theoretically, a company's website should be at the core of an InBound strategy, as it is the most authoritative domain that the organization can control. An intelligent design of the website's information architecture should first identify where audiences are in their buying journey based on the content they consume, and then usher them to advance their journey through a mix of outbound nudges and inbound content.

In general, the InBound model provides all of the correct arguments for why companies need to focus on their inbound channels to attract audiences from search and social media. The model recommends drawing audiences—turning strangers into visitors—through blogs, keywords and social publishing. Once these visitors identify themselves to the company, they become leads in a CRM. At that point, they are contacted through email that nudges them to transact. The method continues beyond the sale, assuming that delighted customers will be compelled to become promoters of the company's brand.

If only it were that simple.

Contrasting InBound with the Content-Centric Model

InBound marketing provides the right steps for the marketing mix, increasing the capabilities of marketing automation software to track and provide specific content based on individual behavior, guiding marketers to navigate the complexities of digital communications technologies and providing a unified dashboard for managing search and social media.

However, the model neglects to cover several important issues. First, InBound only provides a rationale for a series of tactics. It does not provide a smart basis for developing a content or messaging strategy. In fact, it creates reactivity for marketers, as it forces a rigid framework of empty vehicles that need to be filled with content on a regular, ongoing basis.

Second, InBound and other content marketing models recommend generating content and driving people to it. Ideally, they consume the content and change their behavior. However this premise is a gross oversimplification of the customer's buying journey and sets up false assumptions. In the name of customer intimacy, this model completely bypasses the audience's specific needs.

Finally, the biggest drawback in the InBound marketing model is the focus on quantity rather than quality. The InBound methodology suggests that more content will result in more sales. I disagree. Some researchers say that humans now have 8-second attention spans.[33] While the Internet is not a zero-sum game, people's attention has become one. And any model based on the concept of 'more is better' has been partially responsible for our collective content fatigue. Scientists and clinicians can hardly keep up with the scientific discoveries or standards of care in their own fields let alone most marketing content. As we explored in Chapter 1, this content fatigue adversely affects marketing and will soon start to erode the credibility of brands, if not handled diligently.

In contrast, the Content-Centric Model focuses on strategy, building the narrative, imagining the experience and then architecting the tactics. As such,

---

[33] D. Dukette; D. Cornish. *The Essential 20: Twenty Components of an Excellent Health Care Team.* Pittsburgh, PA: RoseDog Books, 2009, pgs. 72–73.

the quantity of content or number of touch-points becomes a function of the strategy and the nuanced needs of the audience and so should the tools required to implement a campaign. Only after those key questions are resolved does it make sense to employ the right technology to attract, convert, sell and delight customers.

Let us now take a tour of how companies have successfully implemented the Content-Centric Model for Marketing Science and Healthcare to create effective digital marketing campaigns.

PART TWO:
Stories

Some people learn through explanation, while others learn through seeing examples of concepts put into real life practice. In Part One, I provided a synthesis of the landscape and described several models that science and medical companies can use to create and deploy effective digital marketing initiatives.

In Part Two, I am deeply honored to share the stories of four companies who have employed the Content-Centric Model for Marketing Science and Healthcare to meet their marketing objectives.

These companies range from small startups to large organizations. Their offerings range from sophisticated technologies to premium consumables. Their objectives vary from launching a product to articulating their value ahead of their Initial Public Offering, and their target audiences vary from laboratory technicians to clinicians in different markets. Yet, these four stories have several key characteristics in common:

1. They all used the Content-Centric Model for Marketing Science and Healthcare to develop their messaging strategy.
2. They all displayed an act of thought leadership.
3. Each campaign orchestrated a catalytic experience.
4. Every company humanized its brand.
5. Most importantly, each team in these companies showed vision, forward thinking and confidence.

I am grateful that my team had an opportunity to participate in the making of each of these stories that have enabled us to learn so much, pour our collective passion into collaborations with smart marketers, to do our best and most creative thinking, and to enjoy the journey along the way. My hope is that these stories will serve as inspiration or guidance as you develop your digital marketing plans.

CHAPTER 4

The New Art of Western Blotting

GE Healthcare Life Sciences

Launching a New Product in a Crowded Market

SYNOPSIS

A new product can disrupt the market. It can also disrupt the status quo of how scientists and clinicians think about a standard technique. Status quo can slow sales. The product launch team must carefully identify specific mental barriers to adoption and systematically lower those barriers within the launch campaign.

In this chapter, I illustrate how an amazing team at GE Healthcare Life Sciences found the underlying barrier to launching an innovative system in a mature, crowded market and how they engineered a communications strategy that lowered these barriers.

This story demonstrates the following techniques:

- The application of the Content-Centric Model to product launches
- Advanced qualitative research analysis that dives deep into understanding the emotions of the target audience
- The creative use of a metaphor without resorting to shallow borrowed interest
- How to signal authority through the subtle use of a spokesperson
- Leveraging documentary-style storytelling as the Catalytic Experience to activate the campaign

The story in this chapter serves as a model of excellence for how the GE Healthcare Life Sciences team deftly navigated the complex landscape of the Western Blotting market.

SHIFTING PERCEPTIONS

"Salty Licorice?" I gasped in surprise. Whenever I travel to a new place, I try to sample the local fare.

I was in Uppsala, Sweden, for 48 hours, consulting with GE Healthcare Life Sciences. At the end of a full day, I asked my hosts to suggest something that represents a local treat that I could taste and take home to California. My hosts told me—and dared me—to try the local black licorice, which they warned me would be quite salty.

As I lay awake at 3:00AM in my hotel room, unable to overcome my jetlag, I reached into the bag of salty, anise-flavored pastilles. I kept trying to shift my own preconceived understanding of how sweet licorice is supposed to taste, so that I could enjoy this savory experience.

All that day, I had been pondering a similar question about another matter.

GE Healthcare Life Sciences was in the midst of preparing to launch a new category of product for Western Blotting, which is a technique invented in the late 1970s for detecting proteins. A well-established protocol for biochemists, Western Blotting is typically a manual, cumbersome and lengthy process. Many complain about its lack of reproducibility, low resolution and high failure rate. The method can take two days without any results, which causes the scientist additional days of detective work to determine whether the negative results are meaningful or whether there was a mistake or artifact in the protocol. It is mostly bench work with a touch of 'voodoo' involved in achieving results. Most scientists say they hate it. As one scientist remarked, "Western Blotting is like petting stray cats."

Since Western Blotting has never been fully systematized, a scientist does not buy a single Western Blotting instrument. Instead, they buy several reagents and bench equipment. The process is analogous to baking bread by hand and sourcing one's own ingredients instead of using a bread machine with its pre-packaged and pre-measured ingredients.

GE Healthcare's Life Sciences division was about to shift how scientists understand Western Blotting. But would scientists let go of their preconceived understanding of how Western Blotting is supposed to be and adopt GE's new Amersham Western Blotting (WB) system?

SITUATION ANALYSIS: THREE SIDES OF THE TRUTH

Company Dynamics—The Company's Side of the Truth

You do not have to conduct many interviews to conclude that most scientists want significant improvement to the workflow, reproducibility, and quantitative power of Western Blotting. Having been one of the providers in traditional Western Blotting products for decades, the product development team at GE Healthcare Life Sciences was all too familiar with scientists' needs.

That is why they decided to create the world's first Western Blotting 'system'—a single instrument that routinizes the Western Blotting workflow and removes many of the manual steps that can introduce user errors, along with a more robust analysis software program that monitors the progress of the workflow and enables more quantifiable results.

While the system logically satisfies the needs that scientists often articulate about Western Blotting, crafting a compelling positioning and value proposition would take far more than merely describing the benefits of the system. As I saw it, we would need to consider three variables to correctly position this product.

First, scientists would have to get used to doing Western Blotting in a machine rather than on a lab bench. A question tugged at me: How disruptive would this new system be in the market? The answer would determine how to position this product to the different audience psychographics within the technology adoption life cycle curve.

Second, the Amersham WB system was not fully automated, meaning that it still required the scientist to move each step of the protocol forward manually. But it was a standardized protocol that aligned, controlled and monitored all of

INNOVATORS
2.5%

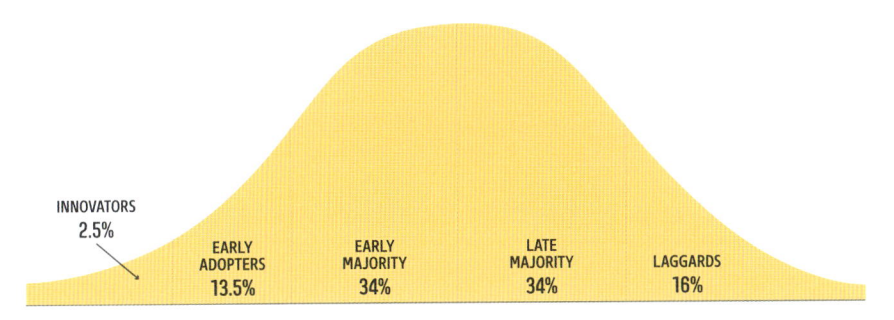

EARLY ADOPTERS
13.5%

EARLY MAJORITY
34%

LATE MAJORITY
34%

LAGGARDS
16%

FIGURE 04.01 The technology adoption life cycle describes the psychographics of customers who adopt new technologies that disrupt their current tools.[34]

the steps within the entire experiment. The system would communicate with the scientist about the progress of each experiment during the run and report any potential issues.

Finally, we had to contend with the fact that GE had a successful franchise that provided excellent tools for the traditional Western Blotting technique, so it would not be wise to focus heavily on the myriad negative associations with traditional Western Blotting.

The team knew that merely articulating the value proposition of the Amersham WB system would not drive the adoption that they expected. If we did not position it well, customers would gloss over the claims and ignore any potential benefit they would achieve through adopting the system, especially given that the cost of such a system was approximately 20 times higher than assembling the pieces and parts for the traditional setup.

We followed the steps of our Content-Centric Marketing Model. First, we needed to lead scientists to recognize they have a need and then educate them about the implications of that need before delivering the value proposition to persuade them.

This launch was going to be tricky. And that is exactly the kind of challenge that my colleagues and I crave at The Linus Group.

---

[34]"Technology Adoption Life Cycle (and curve)." Wikipedia. Accessed online on February 2, 2016, at en.wikipedia.org/wiki/Technology_adoption_life_cycle.

Competitive Dynamics—The Market's Side of the Truth

As mentioned before, the issues with traditional Western Blotting are well-known and well-documented, so it is no wonder that industry providers claim incremental workflow improvements, touting saved time and more reproducible results. In other words, they promise 'faster, cheaper, better' or any combination thereof.

In our research, we identified two classes of competition.

1. **COMPETING CAMPAIGNS:** During the time we prepared to launch the Amersham WB system, we observed no fewer than ten current campaigns with similar claims in the marketplace. The messages canceled each other out by creating white noise in the minds of the audience. We knew we would have to overcome this noise to be successful.

2. **COMPETING TECHNIQUES:** We identified several competing techniques, such as capillary electrophoresis, that were trying to convert scientists away from using Western Blotting towards their own technology. These new systems also touted that they provide faster, more reliable and more quantitative results—but without running Western Blotting itself. On the one hand, these instruments threatened to neutralize the Amersham WB system's value proposition since some claimed a more automated 'sample-in and answer-out' workflow. On the other hand, those new offerings were not based on the operating principles of Western Blotting, which enjoyed 50 years of historical data and required a greater disruption to current scientific workflows. Not only would scientists need to change their workflows, they also had to change their understanding of the operating principles of their technique.

We knew that illuminating an important discrepancy between the scientists' attitudes and their behaviors held the key to successfully launching the system. After researching the market through the lens of the company and analyzing the competitive landscape, we identified the missing piece of the story: Scientists hate Western Blotting, yet the usage of it continued to grow every year. While scientists complained about the lack of reproducibility, they continued to make decisions based on their Western Blotting results. While they complained about a lack of standardization of the protocols, they rarely changed those protocols. The answer we sought would come to us through qualitative market research, which was the third side of the truth.

Customer Dynamics—The Customer's Side of the Truth

Until we take a deep dive into the dynamics of the target customers, no strategy or story can be considered complete. In talking with scientists of all levels and in multiple industries about Western Blotting, we knew we had to wade past the obvious complaints about reproducibility and time-consuming processes in order to find true, actionable insight.

During our fifth target customer interview, an unusual pattern emerged within the course of conversation. Below is an excerpt from a respondent during the qualitative study that we conducted, which led us to an interesting insight.

> **INTERVIEWER** | What are your views about reproducibility in Western Blotting?
>
> **RESPONDENT 11** | *It's a semi-quantitative technique and people are fooling themselves and the entire scientific community… My personal experience for 20 years that I have in Western Blotting is that they're not very reproducible or accurate.*
>
> …5 minutes later…
>
> **INTERVIEWER** | So in your lab, how do you contend with this problem of reproducibility with your Western Blots?
>
> **RESPONDENT 11** | *I wouldn't say we have a problem with Western Blots.*

At first, it seems that the respondent is contradicting herself. However, reviewing the dialogue again reveals a subtle and powerful nuance. In the first exchange, she is complaining about the technique in general. However, she reports no problem with her own technique when the conversation shifts to her personal use of Western Blotting.

In interview after interview, this theme manifested itself in similar ways—yet the pattern was quite clear. If you ask about Western Blotting in general, then the typical diatribe about reproducibility and time-consuming processes will follow. If you ask about the scientist's own Western Blot process, then they say everything is fine.

The Full Story

This observation became central to our understanding of how to enter the market for GE's Amersham WB system. Western Blotting is one of the few remaining techniques where biochemists still have physical contact with their science.

> Western Blotting is a technique that requires artistry to master—and that artistry is a point of pride for a scientist.

The mastery is not documented in standard protocols. Instead, it is passed from scientist to scientist through the ancient tradition of apprenticeship. Scientists have a love-hate relationship with Western Blots. If they do them, they master the art. And it satisfies a scientist's sense of self-expression—to amass and to bestow knowledge.

CREATING THE BACKBONE OF THE STORY

Positioning the Amersham WB System

Synthesizing the three sides of the truth about the Western Blotting market from our situation analysis process, the positioning for the Amersham WB system became quite clear.

Formal Positioning Statement

> *For* Scientists frequently using Western Blot as a standard technique to detect the presence and quantity of proteins
>
> *Who need* to get more decisive insights out of each sample and each experiment in order to succeed in today's increasingly competitive research environment.
>
> *Amersham's WB system* is the world's first fully integrated Western Blot system
>
> Providing standardization in the separation, transfer, detection and quantitative analysis of proteins.

Unlike traditional Western Blot protocols that are not quantitative and provide no way of monitoring progress during the time-consuming protocol,

Only GE's Amersham WB system integrates standard steps, aligning the steps with software that quantifies results while monitoring the steps of the protocol and alerting the user of the progress of each step.

We distilled the positioning and these insights into a value proposition synopsis that captured the essence of what GE provides to the market:

Value Proposition

The most consistent Western Blot data, every sample, every time.

The GE Amersham WB system minimizes assay variability to achieve quantifiable data from every sample, every time. Data normalization combined with a standardized and monitored process, every step of the way, to get more out of each blot. With fewer repeat experiments and controls, scientists will remain in control of their science and realize their true potential.

BUILDING THE STORY: THE CONTENT-CENTRIC MESSAGING STRATEGY

As marketers and sales professionals know, there is nothing like a well-crafted and mass orchestrated value proposition to make a market roll its eyes.

Even though we crafted a solution that seemed to resolve the challenges we faced in bringing the Amersham WB system to market, we needed to create an arc for the narrative that would adhere to the content-centric marketing principles outlined in *Persuading Scientists* and outlined in Chapter 3 of this book.

GE's story needed to usher the audience through a three-part journey that created: 1) Recognition around a need, then encouraged 2) Exploration of the possible paths available, and then motivated them to undergo 3) Evaluation of the commercial options available to fulfill the need.

Through this narrative, we aimed to condition the audience to adopt a frame of reference so that they can accept GE's value proposition—and we would shape

PHASE	RECOGNITION	EXPLORATION	EVALUATION
	Leadership	**Education**	**Persuasion**
MESSAGE	Western Blotting (WB) has too much variability and no standardization.	Standardization does not need to compete with your artistry.	The Amersham WB system enables the standardization of Western Blotting.
NARRATIVE	Western Blotting is an art and requires mastery beyond merely following protocol. Scientists gain this mastery through time and experience, but this comes at a great cost. It keeps scientists' energy on the manual process and the unimportant.	By routinizing the manual steps, scientists will become free to continue focusing on their own mastery and on their own art, giving them more control over their experiments.	The Amersham WB system standardizes all of the manual steps in Western Blotting and employs a software system to monitor progress, giving the scientist the ability to make more progress on their science.

market perception while distinguishing the product in a noisy sea of sameness. As you can see, the story first provokes the scientist to recognize that part of their focus remains mired in the unimportant aspects of Western Blotting. The story progresses by educating them to think differently about where they should focus their intellectual power and their artistry—and that creates the correct framework for GE to deliver its value proposition for the system.

This campaign needed to be highly experiential in order to be believable, so the campaign architecture was critical to success. As marketers, we are in the business of shifting understanding of the market, and the most powerful way that audiences will believe the story is if they experience it. And it is far more important for a story to be believed than told.

THE MIRACLE OF CREATIVE: DEMONSTRATING THE MESSAGE

For us, campaign architecture is the beginning of developing creative.[35] Recall that our situation analysis revealed several barriers that marketing needed to

---

[35] In the marketing industry, the word 'creative' is used as a noun, and refers to the deliverable of providing look and feel, tone and texture to the campaign. Most traditionally, it comprises the art and copywriting of a campaign initiative. From our perspective at The Linus Group, this is a highly narrowed view of creative, as it should comprise the campaign architecture, story and experiences.

overcome in order for GE to be successful in entering the market with the Amersham WB system. Each phase of the story provided its own set of barriers that the campaign needed to overcome. As you can see from Figure 04.02 (page 73), the campaign needed to do some heavy lifting—and that was a tall order given the myriad barriers that threatened our success.

PHASE	RECOGNITION	EXPLORATION	EVALUATION
INVOKING	CREATIVITY	HYPOTHESIS	VALIDATION
	Leadership	Education	Persuasion
MESSAGE	Western Blotting is not a black box. It requires artistry from every scientist.	Western Blotting requires standardization but not to compete with artistry.	The Amersham WB system enables scientists to apply their artistry to their science.
OBJECTIVES	Substantiate claim that scientists are spending their energy focusing on tweaks, tips and tricks in order to get good quality Western Blots. Strengthen the entire GE Healthcare Life Sciences portfolio of traditional Western Blotting products.	Demonstrate that systemizing Western Blotting will not limit the scientist's tactile connection with their science. In fact, it will increase their ability to 'be the artist.'	Illustrate how the Amersham WB system is exactly the same as the current Western Blotting workflow, just systematized to overcome any barriers that may exist in moving from individual components to a system.
BARRIERS	As a supplier, GE can't directly make this claim, because it will not be deemed credible.	Scientists will see standardization as a black box, threatening their connection with, and control over, their sample.	Scientists would have no visual reference to make the connection between their traditional Western Blotting equipment and a 'system.'
STRATEGY	Create an experience that invites scientists to demonstrate that producing reproducible Western Blots requires folk knowledge.	Show an analogy of another art form where artists were first resistant to technological change but found greater possibility by embracing the change.	Introduce the system through the lens of the Western Blotting workflow, instead of the typical specifications or feature-benefit discourse of an instrument.
SOLUTION	A Virtual Western Blot Experiment that appeals to scientists to display their artistry by sharing their 'Tips and Tricks' to produce a great Western Blot.	Show the evolution of photography from analog to digital and compare it with the evolution of Western Blotting, making the case that the standardization of Western Blotting will increase the artistry of scientists.	Leverage the same graphical interpretation of the Virtual Western Blot Experiment as a digital brochure for the Amersham WB system, providing features, benefits and multimedia content for each phase of the workflow, rather than the system.

THE CATALYTIC EXPERIENCE—
LEVERAGING STORYTELLING

A review of the strategy made clear that launching the Amersham WB system would require more than a content blitz. Instead, we needed to choreograph the conversation with the market and roll out each phase of the messaging strategy in chronological order.[36] We needed to create an intricate media plan that assigned outbound vehicles for each phase of the message.

1. LEADERSHIP

Leadership Inbound—First, our creative team developed an interactive infographic that emulated every step of a typical Western Blot protocol. We provided an interesting fact for each step and asked a key question about how the audience optimizes their own protocol during each step.

Leadership Outbound—Our media partner, *The Scientist*, has grown a fantastic audience within its social channels. We worked with them to develop a set of Facebook posts (Figure 04.03, page 74) that invited scientists to share their tips, tricks and sentiments about Western Blotting.

Leadership Results—In a four-week period, it was clear that we had succeeded in delivering our Leadership message. With an almost exclusive mix of paid and earned outreach on social media channels (mainly Facebook and Twitter), we received close to 10,000 unique visitors to the Virtual Western Blotting Interactive Infographic and received thousands of interactions. En masse, the scientific community with whom we engaged documented the message we wanted to portray—that the traditional Western Blot experiment requires nuance and is highly variable.

---

[36]The decision to roll out each phase of the messaging strategy as discrete, chronological campaigns, or to roll out the entire campaign at once, depends upon whether or not the market needs to be predisposed to a new way of thinking before the introduction of a solution. If you sense too much headwind, or if the launch date of your product is uncertain and you need to develop a teaser campaign, then it may make sense to launch the messaging strategy in phases. Otherwise, I recommend developing and launching every phase of the messaging strategy at once, to enable your audience to navigate each phase based on their own terms.

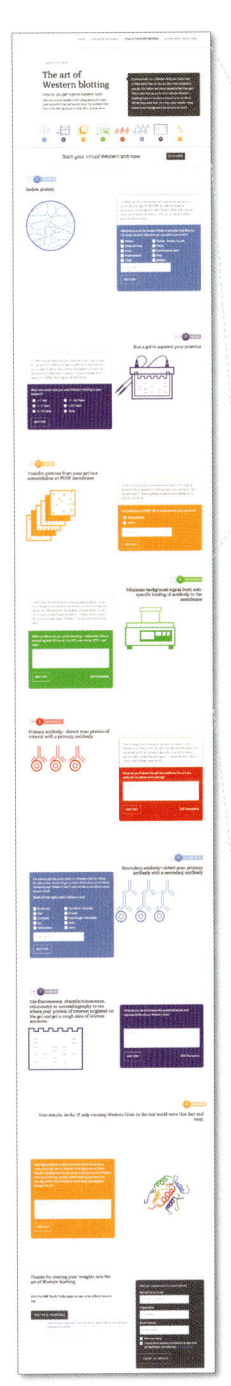

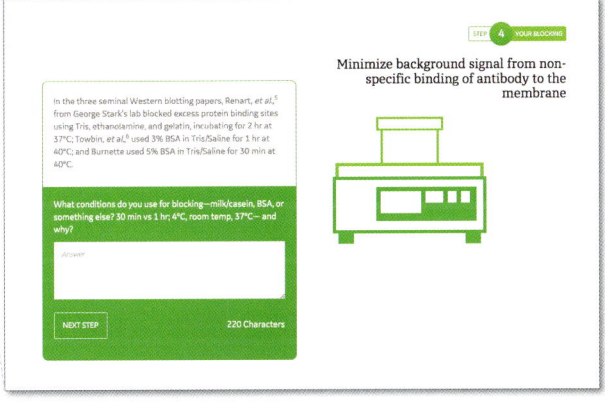

FIGURE 04.02 The interactive infographic of a virtual Western Blot experiment uses highly stylized icons that depict each step of the traditional Western Blotting experiment. Using a long-scroll design, the infographic encourages the user to interact with every stage of the experiment by asking for input. This technique produces a subtle-but-powerful conditioning effect that trains the user to provide information at each stage. This creates trust. When the user arrives at the bottom of the page, she is encouraged to provide contact information. As you will see in the subsequent figures, this same iconography is used throughout to give the impression that the Amersham WB system is a continuous innovation—rather than disruptive—to the traditional technique.[37]

---

[37]GE Healthcare Life Sciences. "The art of Western blotting." Accessed online on February 4, 2016, at https://promo.gelifesciences.com/gl/artofwesternblotting/workflow.html.

CATALYTIC EXPERIENCES | 73

FIGURE 04.03 A series of posts shared through the popular Facebook page for *The Scientist* generated millions of impressions and drew a tremendous amount of social engagement. The above example is only one post, garnering over 450 shares and 665 likes (which increase the post's reach to new audiences). This type of 'advertising' is highly quantifiable and effective.[38]

2. EDUCATION

Education Inbound—At this stage, we pivoted the campaign and invited scientists to entertain the idea of evolving their Western Blotting workflows. Here, we leveraged the use of analogy as a powerful scaffold for demonstrating the possibility of change while addressing the fear that many scientists would experience—whether or not they could articulate that fear.

We chose the evolution of photography from film-based to digital modalities as the analogy. Although this analogy is slightly cliché, it proved to be ideal for several reasons:

1. We wanted to connect Western Blotting to an art, given the 'mastery' that many scientists felt they had achieved in perfecting their Western Blotting technique.

2. When new, the idea of digital photography created a negative reaction within the fine art photography community, who initially feared losing tactile control over their art. Later, this community realized gains in creative freedom with the new tools.

---

[38] *The Scientist*, Facebook page post, July 25, 2014. Accessed online on February 2, 2016, at www.facebook.com/TheScientistMagazine/photos/a.216622478361000.54773.212009668822281/771125802910662/?type=3&theater.

We created a second infographic, comparing the evolution of Western Blotting to the evolution of photography, and focused on the final step between the two techniques.

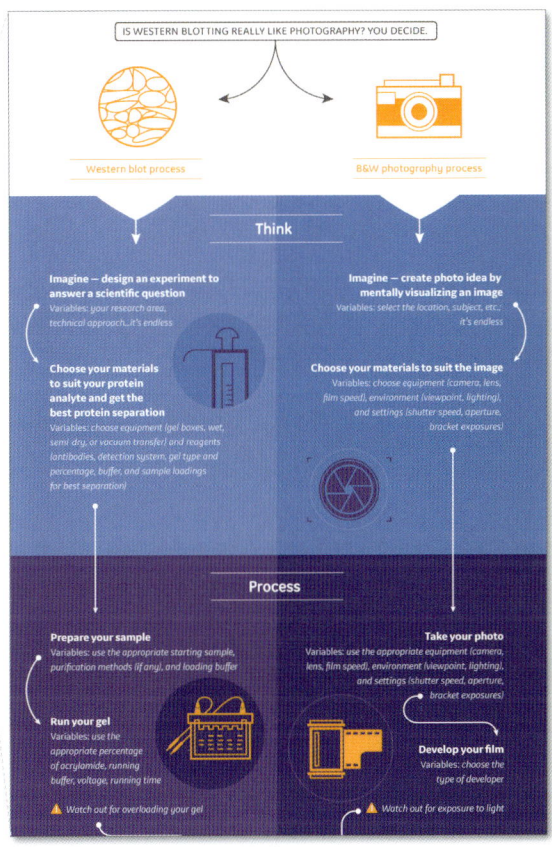

FIGURE 04.04 The long-scroll infographic that depicts the evolution of Western Blotting focuses on the obvious lack of standardization of the technique. The comparison to the evolution of photography starts at the top, showing parallel advances in both techniques in the middle of the infographic. By the time the user reaches the bottom of the page, the stark difference between the evolutions of the two techniques becomes clear where digital photography has standardized the process but Western Blotting remains highly manual.[39]

[39] GE Healthcare Life Sciences. "The art of Western blotting." Accessed online on February 4, 2016, at https://promo.gelifesciences.com/gl/artofwesternblotting/info.html?extcmp=K14097-GL-inteml-webinar4_share.

CATALYTIC EXPERIENCES | 75

Education Outbound—Metaphor or analogy is often used as a creative vehicle to illustrate a particular point, but sometimes the analogy fails to make the connection with its intended audience. We wanted to introduce the journey that artists took in their adoption of digital photography as an analogy to encourage scientists to see themselves on the same journey. Therefore, we needed to introduce the analogy through the context of a scientific conversation.

In collaboration with *Science* magazine, a media partner, we assembled a panel of scientists for a webinar to discuss 'tips and tricks' related to Western Blotting. *Science* excels at its sponsored webinars and has consistently garnered a large audience for them. One of the panelists, who was a scientist at GE Healthcare and an amateur photographer, was our key catalyst on the panel.

We requested that the GE scientist casually introduce the analogy during the panel discussion portion of the webinar. He did so in a natural way. A few days after the webinar, we sent an outbound message to the registrants and several in-house and purchased lists, referencing the GE scientist's analogy of the evolution of Western Blotting as similar to the advent of digital photography—and invited the audience to study in greater depth the infographic that illustrated the similarities.

It was a pitch-perfect duet to introduce a creative theme for the campaign, delivered through a credible channel by our credible scientist—and through casual, scientific discussion.

Introducing the campaign's main creative idea through casual conversation deliberately minimized any pretense that may have rendered the idea as too contrived. On the other hand, the swift follow-up demonstrated the level of dedication and commitment that GE Healthcare Life Sciences had towards its audience and the market at large.

Up to this point, we were fully engaged in preconditioning the market and had not yet mentioned any product offering. Since we had established the Leadership and Education messages, it was time to tie the campaign together through our final step of Persuasion Messaging.

3. PERSUASION

Persuasion Inbound—On September 30, 2014, scientists would be introduced to a new way of obtaining their Western Blots—a far more standardized, mechanized and reproducible way.

The final content prepared for Amersham WB system's product launch tied the entire storyline together. By first demonstrating that traditional Western Blotting was highly variable and required folk knowledge, and then assuaging scientists' potential fears of losing control or mastery over their science, we had earned the right to deliver our value proposition—that the Amersham WB system was the new standard in Western Blotting.

We added this third and final module to the microsite and developed a new home page design that provided a complete user experience for each module of the story.

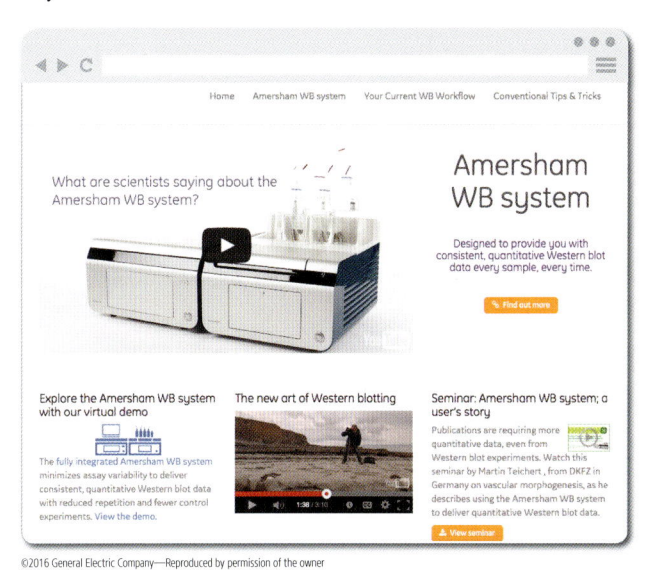

FIGURE 04.05 Upon the launch of the Amersham WB system, the Persuasion Messaging dominated the user experience, but the complete narrative was told through all of the key content. The redesigned landing page prominently featured the product and a video that was designed to be the Catalytic Experience within the campaign, tying the overall story of Western Blotting and photography together.[40]

---

[40] GE Healthcare Life Sciences. "The art of Western blotting." Accessed online on February 4, 2016, at https://promo.gelifesciences.com/gl/artofwesternblotting/home.html.

CATALYTIC EXPERIENCES | 77

"The thing that really drives me is more informative ways to ask a question."

"The most important part of the process is designing the experiment right."

"I always looked at Western Blotting in a very similar way to photography."

"Any technique that takes a lot of time because it's got a lot of manual processing, the chances of you making a mistake are even higher."

"There are some elements that you can control, and then there are some elements that are more difficult to control."

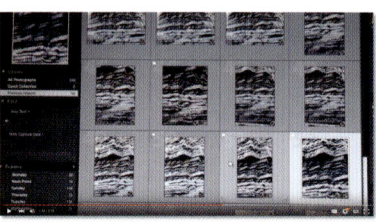

"Digital photography has changed the whole process. What it hasn't done is taken any of the artistry out."

"If you have a machine that standardizes the process and takes out the human errors, then you trust the data you're getting..."

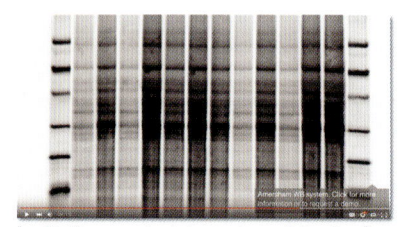

"...and that frees up your time to do more science and better science."

©2016 General Electric Company—Reproduced by permission of the owner

FIGURE 04.06 The launch of the Amersham WB system featured a documentary-style video of the campaign's scientist spokesperson, who demonstrated the parallels between Western Blotting and fine-art photography. The spokesperson provided the key shortcomings of the scientific technique, dispelled fears of change and then introduced the value proposition of the new instrument. His scientific rigor and authority was balanced by his calculated and gentle tone as well as his creative expression of photography.[41]

---

[41]GE Healthcare Life Sciences. "The art of Western blotting... Time for a change." Accessed online via YouTube on February 4, 2016, at youtu.be/fMyXNz81-cM.

The Catalytic Experience in this campaign occurred within the Persuasion Messaging: a three-minute documentary-style video featuring our spokesperson—the same GE scientist and hobbyist photographer from the *Science* webinar—who delivered the complete narrative through the creative analogy of photography. This video brings narrative and personality to the entire campaign while our scientist delivers several key 'learning moments.' First, he draws a parallel between photography and Western Blotting, articulating the common pitfall of the two techniques. Later, he draws another parallel between the evolution of photography and the evolution of Western Blotting with the Amersham WB system. Leveraging documentary-style storytelling, we were able to deliver the entire arc of the Content-Centric Marketing Model messaging strategy in an engaging, experiential form. Figure 04.06 illustrates the key frames from the video and the narration that delivers the main 'learning moments' from the story.

Instead of the standard static brochure, we developed an interactive collateral experience for the Amersham WB system, using the same flow and iconography from the Virtual Western Blotting Experiment. This allowed us to draw subtle parallels between the traditional workflow that all protein scientists are used to experiencing. We believed this would lower the barrier for adoption.

We leveraged our best practices for lead generation and placed forms with calls-to-action throughout key sections of the microsite in order to maximize conversion.

Persuasion Outbound—In order to build anticipation for the launch, we choreographed an online unveiling event. We invited the leads we had generated to date and sent invitations to others through third-party channels. The event featured several beta users of the instrument who discussed the standardization that they had achieved in their Western Blotting, and it featured key benefits of the Amersham WB system. The event was housed on the microsite, where we encouraged respondents to further explore content about Western Blotting standardization and GE's new system. We published and

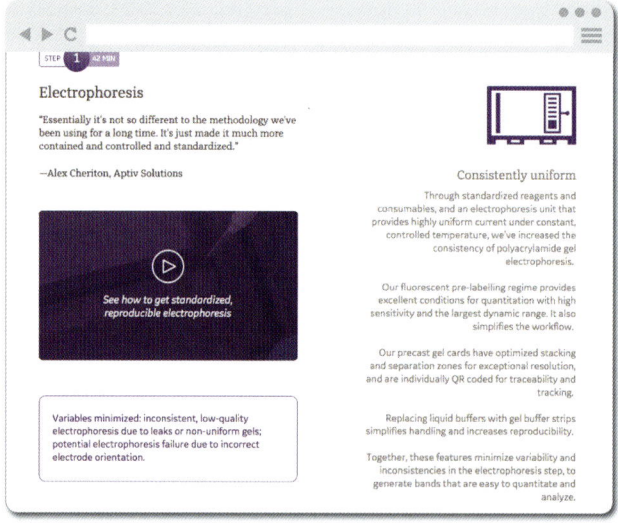

FIGURE 04.07 By leveraging the same flow and iconography of the interactive infographic that depicted the traditional Western Blotting workflow, this interactive product collateral walked through each stage of the Western Blotting experiment. It showed short vignettes of the instrument and delivered the new steps through the lens of the familiar workflow. This juxtaposition signaled continuous innovation and aimed to lower barriers to adoption.[42]

shared the video of the event via social media and YouTube in order to drive viewership and traffic to the microsite and ultimately the lead generation process. In this way, we tied all of the content pieces together to drive leads.

THE OUTCOME

The advantage of working from a platform is that one can anticipate the metrics for each phase of the program in order to monitor and optimize each effort in real time. Thus, we evaluate campaigns in terms of the effort it takes to reach our target instead of success or failure.

The table in Figure 04.08 illustrates anticipated versus actual performance for each phase of the campaign.

---

[42]GE Healthcare Life Sciences. "What if Western blots worked the same way every time, quantitatively?" Accessed online on February 4, 2014, at https://promo.gelifesciences.com/gl/artofwesternblotting/sales-tools.html.

TOTAL PERFORMANCE

Media Budget	$200,000	Total Targeted Traffic	94,000	Total Targeted Engagement	2,200
Planned Budget	$183,680	Total Planned Traffic	156,421	Total Planned Engagement	4,032
Remaining	$616,320	Surplus	531,682	Surplus	13,927

PERFORMANCE FOR EACH PHASE

LEADERSHIP		EDUCATION		PERSUASION	
1. Drive Engagement to Post Stories and Viewership of Interactive Workflow. 2. Support Registrations and Viewership of *Science* Magazine Webinar.		Drive Viewership of the Photography Infographic.		1. Drive Registrations to Global Webcast Introducing the Product. 2. Drive Viewership of the Interactive Demo and Request Demo (Lead).	
Target Clicks	40,000	Target Clicks	14,000	Target Clicks	40,000
Target Engagement	400			Target Demo Requests	600
Science Webinar Reg.	1,500			Target Webinar Reg.	1,200
Actual Clicks	24,614	Actual Clicks	18,086	Actual Clicks	113,721
Actual Engagement	441			Actual Engagement	3,238

FIGURE 04.08 It is easy to become entranced by marketing performance data, but it is critical to maintain focus on the overall objectives when reviewing metrics. For example, we did not see the expected number of intended impressions in the campaign's Leadership phase. However, the campaign over-performed in total engagement, which was the main goal for this phase.[43]

As we reviewed the campaign's final performance with our colleagues in Uppsala, we remembered the pre-conditioning we had done in order to earn the right to deliver the Amersham WB system's value proposition. And, as I reached into my bag to grab the last piece of salty licorice purchased during my visit to Uppsala, I noticed I had also been converted by a new experience—and, now, actually craved the complex flavors of the Swedish treat.

---

[43]Note: While the ratios have been kept the same, the actual numbers have been changed.

CHAPTER 5

We Are All Connected

―

Invitae

Activating a Brand

SYNOPSIS

How do you become a leader? You can talk about yourself and how awesome you are. Or you earn the title by acting as a servant to the community you are trying to lead.

There are few concepts as overplayed and misunderstood as branding, and in the science and medical fields, branding is typically reduced to the creation of an appealing 'look-and-feel' and the consistent application of a logo, colors, fonts and other form factor elements. Unfortunately, most companies stop there. From my perspective, developing the form factor is just the starting line for effectively generating awareness and preference for a brand. Brand is an important pillar in a company's ethos next to its mission, core values and strategy.

This chapter is a story about courage. It is about how the dynamic startup Invitae articulated its brand by taking a definitive stance in a fast-paced and crowded market. Guided by the Content-Centric Marketing Model, the company attracted attention from its diverse audiences.

In this chapter, I will discuss the following:
- The right time for a startup company to commit to a brand position
- Application of the Content-Centric Model to brand campaigns
- How to earn leadership through serving the community
- Breathing new life into an existing brand, without the expense and hassle of changing the logo

The story portrayed in this chapter illustrates that the Invitae brand is more than a mere abstraction of a faceless, voiceless entity. It is a group of people driven by their passion and values.

TO BRAND OR TO BE BRANDED

Invitae's business strategy is a long-play. It is among the few companies that are truly and sincerely guided by a vision of what the future can become—and needs to become—for the world to be a better, healthier place for all of us. The company's leadership has a multi-stage strategy to realize this vision, and they are making steady progress toward this reality.

In 2014, after having dialed in its technology, offerings and operations, Invitae was ready to ramp up its presence in the world. The company's leaders wanted to emerge as a fully formed entity, with a complete story and a hard-hitting value proposition. They were also preparing for an Initial Public Offering (IPO) and needed to tell the story of their vision and multi-stage strategy to another skeptical audience: the investment community.

The trouble was—as is often the case with startup companies—Invitae needed to stay nimble enough to test various iterations of its story and value proposition in the rapidly-evolving landscape of the genetic testing market. Following the traditional branding route in expending disproportionate energy in researching, crafting and validating a functional value proposition and translating that to a rigid brand system would not have been a wise investment for Invitae at that time.

The old adage from Aristotle, who said "nature abhors a vacuum,"[44] provided the team with final guidance on how to proceed. Brand, or be branded. As soon as a brand makes a public appearance, it starts to amass impressions. If the brand image is undefined or under-defined, its audience will define it in their own minds, and the brand becomes hijacked by the community, or worse, by competitors. Many startups make this mistake and expose the market to

---

[44]"Horror vacui (physics)." Wikipedia. Accessed online on February 14, 2016, at en.wikipedia.org/wiki/Horror_vacui_(physics).

their undefined brand in the name of nimbleness or for the romantic notion of early-stage bootstrapping. The consequences end up being far too costly to repair later because companies have to first undo any unwanted associations with their brand just to arrive at a blank canvas on which to paint their desired image. The leadership team at Invitae knew the perils of under-defining their brand, and was not about to jeopardize its vision in this way.

This presented an interesting challenge: how to activate the Invitae brand and sharpen its value proposition while creating a brand system that still enabled Invitae to be nimble in its market. We turned the challenge into an opportunity and built it into the project brief itself.

With this brief in hand, we began our collaboration with Invitae to build a brand that supported its story, no matter where it was on the journey to realize its vision.

SITUATION ANALYSIS: THREE SIDES OF THE TRUTH

Company Dynamics—The Company's Side of the Truth

Genetic testing is an exciting new market for many businesses and represents a growth area in the healthcare landscape. Massive advancement in sequencing technologies and recent regulatory approvals on standard testing assays are making it easier for labs to obtain at least the raw data about a patient's genetics.

Not to belittle the massive technological complexities of analyzing and reporting a genetic test, but given the many complexities of the genetic testing market and the countless questions that need to be answered, technology is almost the easy part. The more challenging—and frankly exciting—questions that Invitae needed to answer were around its business strategy: Who is the customer today and who will it be tomorrow? What do these customers need today and tomorrow? What is the true benefit of Invitae's offering, and how will it differentiate from the rest of the market to succeed. You know, *positioning*.

As of this writing, the genetic testing market is the most exciting, fast-paced and rapidly shifting landscape in the entire industry. To say that the market is in the early-adopter phase is an understatement. Everyone considers himself a visionary. Everyone is simultaneously your collaborator and your competitor. With a diverse set of actors ranging from patients, their families and their healthcare providers all the way to investors, regulators, lawmakers and ethicists, it is difficult to even determine whom to define as your 'audience.' It almost feels that the traditional rules of marketing don't apply. But don't they?

Every aspect of the market presents ambiguities, from evolving regulatory guidelines to Supreme Court rulings on the validity of patents; from questions about the clinical utility of the genetic information obtained through the tests, to questions about who should pay and who should own the data. Confusion exists at every turn. To a very few, who have the right mix of a vision, passion and courage, this tumultuous market is full of opportunity. The founders and leaders of Invitae are among these few.

Invitae's founders started the company with a grand vision: that providing genetic information to people will make the world better, safer and healthier. In order for this to become reality, billions of people need to gain access to their genetic information, own their information and leverage their information to make better health, lifestyle and economic decisions about their lives.

Invitae sees genetic information as a new currency in the 21st century and the information that connects humanity in new ways. Invitae also thinks that genetic information is, and will be, increasingly valuable to an individual's life—and so trust is a major factor in people's decisions to obtain their genetic information. People will wonder whom to trust to sequence and store their precious genetic information.

Trust is earned, not granted. That is why Invitae began its journey by supporting a patient's existing trusting healthcare relationship--the relationship between patient and care provider. Instead of looking for novel genetic markers in order to gain differentiation, Invitae decided that its initial offering would be to aggregate all of the known and medically-actionable genetic markers onto a single assay and provide a flexible test menu to care providers. This offer would have a single price for any gene or every gene and a fast turn-around of less than two weeks. The company's original tagline, "Reinventing Genetic Testing," aimed to communicate its unique offering while hinting at the company's depth and journey to something greater. However, Invitae's brand and initial communications were bare and lacked the texture to effectively signal the depth and richness that the company was building.

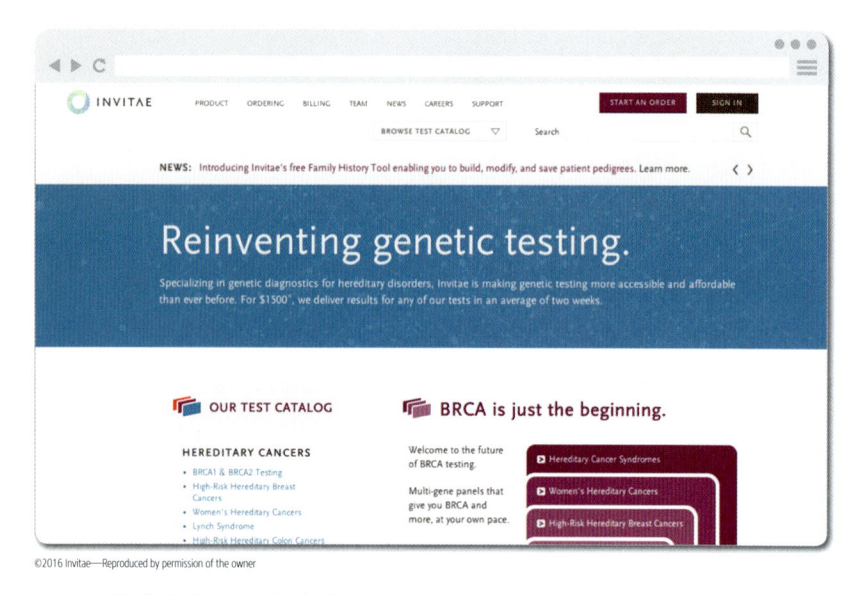

FIGURE 05.01 The 'before' picture of Invitae's brand as seen on its website in January 2014, revealed a beautiful core identity, but with minimal support from texture and richness to fully articulate the company's ethos.[45]

The company knew focusing on genetic diagnostic tests would be a good starting place, but it needed a story that was much bigger, because every day another entrant was aggressively competing on price, turn-around time and the test-menu. The competition was fierce and saturating the market at an alarming rate. While Invitae had no intention of being reactive to competitive forces, ignoring them altogether would not be wise.

---

[45]Invitae website. Accessed online on January 20, 2014, at www.invitae.com. The Invitae logo and all graphics represented in this chapter are trademarks or registered trademarks of Invitae. Reproduced with permission of the owner.

Competitive Dynamics—The Market's Side of the Truth

In order to understand the tumultuous competitive landscape, there are two key companies, and events that transpired around them, which shaped the overall competitive landscape for Invitae: 23andMe and Myriad Genetics.

23andMe

In the early 2000s, 23andMe started with the mission to provide genetic information to people. Reasoning that genetic information belongs to individuals, the company adopted a direct-to-consumer strategy, which accelerated the adoption of the consumer genetics industry. Through a mail-order kit, consumers could supply a saliva sample, which 23andMe analyzed. Customers could log into a community portal to access information about their ancestry, as well as information about their health.

This latter part of the information that 23andMe provided raised concerns from many healthcare professionals who were being cut out of the loop, as well as the U.S. Food and Drug Administration (FDA). In November 2013, the FDA ordered 23andMe to stop providing health information because it claimed that the company's product was classified as a diagnostic 'device' and needed proper clinical trial validation and FDA approvals.[46] Since then, 23andMe has been working with the FDA, and regulatory bodies in other countries, to continue providing more expansive health-related information.

As of June 2015, 23andMe had provided genetic information to over 1,000,000 consumers.[47] More importantly, the company pioneered a global discussion about the ownership of genetic information that forced the issue with many groups, including the need for regulators to update their guidelines regarding the questions surrounding safety and diagnosis of disease versus genetic propensity.

---

[46] U.S. Food and Drug Administration. "Warning Letter to 23andMe." Accessed online on February 14, 2016, at www.fda.gov/ICECI/EnforcementActions/WarningLetters/2013/ucm376296.htm.
[47] 23andME. "Power of One Million." Accessed online on February 16, 2016, at blog.23andme.com/news/one-in-a-million/.

For Invitae, these events provided them with a blueprint of how to enter the market and support the overall discourse about genetics, but also to build trust along the way. But the question still remained, who owns your genes?

Myriad Genetics

As an early pioneer in complex genetic testing, Myriad Genetics patented a genetic signature from a mutation within the BRCA gene, which has been found to have a high correlation to breast cancer in most women and some men, as well as other types of cancer. Not only was the BRCA test a powerful diagnostic tool for possible treatment options, it also provided actionable risk assessment and preventative measures for people and families with a history of breast cancer. The power of BRCA testing would enter the public spotlight with Angelina Jolie's news that she tested positive for BRCA and had decided to take preventive measures.[48] Less than a month after Ms. Jolie's news, the Supreme Court would invalidate Myriad Genetics' patent to the BRCA mutation, and the company would lose exclusivity in providing this test.[49]

The growing popularity of the BRCA test, coupled with the Supreme Court ruling on Myriad Genetics' patent, resulted in a feeding frenzy for genetic testing companies to try to grab valuable market share by providing tests at lower costs and with faster turnaround times than Myriad. Overnight, the genetic testing market transformed from an intellectual-property-driven business to a service-business. But what Myriad still owned was the largest database of tests performed on the most diverse population of patients, which directly translated to the accuracy of the company's bioinformatics and the confidence in its results.

Given this onslaught of laboratories empowered with the democratization of technology to grab market share, Invitae needed to enter the mainstream market as a leader. What better way to earn leadership than by serving the community you are trying to lead? To know how to serve them, we would need to understand their sentiments.

---

[48] A. Jolie. "My Medical Choice." *The New York Times*, May 14, 2013. Accessed online on February 16, 2016, at nyti.ms/18iuMgh.
[49] U.S. Supreme Court. "Syllabus: Association for Molecular Pathology et al. v. Myriad Genetics, Inc., et al." Accessed online on February 16, 2016, at https://www.supremecourt.gov/opinions/12pdf/12-398_1b7d.pdf.

Customer Dynamics—The Customer's Side of the Truth

Given Invitae's initial strategy to support the trusted relationship between patients and their care providers, the team focused on clinicians and genetic counselors as the initial target audience. A research study, which included a series of in-depth interviews with these target audiences, revealed three specific anxieties about the changing landscape of genetic testing.

First, the complexities of genetic testing results challenge the 'differential diagnosis' method that has been standard practice since the early 20th century.[50] Physicians have been taught to gather evidence to form a hypothesis about a patient's condition before systematically eliminating options to formulate a diagnosis. However, genetic tests provide a complicated picture of interdependent data-points, forcing the care provider to completely change the way that they diagnose. While groups such as the American College of Medical Genetics & Genomics (ACMG) are working with the medical community to provide guidance and standards, the vast majority of hard-working, everyday care providers simply do not know how to change their practice in a way that helps them stay ahead of their patients' growing knowledge about genetically-driven decisions.

Second, we uncovered ambiguities about a care provider's responsibility when reading a patient's genetic test and accidentally diagnosing an unrelated condition or an early propensity for a condition that could significantly change a patient's life. Imagine a healthy patient deciding to get a full genome profile in order to determine his risk of hereditary cancers due to family history, only to find that he has a mutation that may lead to Huntington's disease, a neurodegenerative disorder for which there is currently no cure or effective treatment.[51] While care providers are much more comfortable with a non-genetic corollary (e.g., a chest X-ray to diagnose pneumonia may detect the presence of lung cancer), the concept of looking into a patient's genetics is much more complicated and far more scary.

---

[50] "Differential Diagnosis." Wikipedia. Accessed online on February 16, 2016, at en.wikipedia.org/wiki/Differential_diagnosis.
[51] "Huntington's Disease." Wikipedia. Accessed online on February 16, 2016, at en.wikipedia.org/wiki/Huntington%27s_disease.

Third, genetic testing is currently associated with the detection or diagnosis of disease, a time of great fear and anxiety for most patients and for some care providers. This fear was never more prominently exemplified than in an in-depth interview we conducted with a physician, who began by saying how much he loved genetics and believed in patients owning their genetic information to help make the right decisions. Through the course of the conversation, we discussed the implications of genetic testing. At the end, we asked the physician if he would get his own genetic profile—and he said no. He said he would rather not know. This is the same physician who said he is a complete proponent of getting genetic information.

In order for the world to embrace genetic testing, we needed to shift the understanding of what such information can mean and to create positive associations between genetic information and healthy living.

The Full Story

Synthesizing the three sides of the truth, we had a truly actionable insight.

> People need to love their genetics rather than fear them.

With this core common truth shared by Invitae with the world, we had all of the necessary insight we needed to position Invitae and correctly activate its brand.

CREATING THE BACKBONE OF THE STORY

Positioning Invitae

With our insights, we created the following formal positioning for Invitae. Positioning statements are not meant to be customer-facing language, and they are especially challenging to write when trying to position a brand, compared with the 'Golden Circle' model. However, they still serve as a pivotal document to help the team align on the specifics of the strategy.

Formal Positioning Statement

For care providers and their patients

Who need to overcome their fears and anxieties about the complexities of adopting genetic testing

Invitae
Provides the most trusted path to order, interpret, deliver results and pay for genetic tests

Unlike other test providers who focus on menu, accuracy, price or turn-around time

Only Invitae is working to gain acceptance of genetic testing by connecting communities (e.g., patients, care providers, payers) together, rather than treating them in silos.

As a matter of exercise, we also distilled the essence of Invitae's positioning into a value proposition line. (Again, remember that a value proposition statement is still internally-facing language and not meant to serve as a tagline or a headline.):

Value Proposition

The most trusted provider of genetic testing.

As the team aligned around the strategy, it was time to craft the narrative.

BUILDING THE STORY: THE CONTENT-CENTRIC MESSAGING STRATEGY

The most powerful brands are honest distillations of the core of a company. Said differently, a successful branding initiative will allow the company's truest form to be displayed and celebrated. Anything additional to this core truth would be distorting the company's image into something that is inauthentic. This is the reason why most brands come across as shallow, trite or disingenuous.

To breathe meaning into a brand, you need great stories. And many times great stories arise from a bold stance about an issue. In a market that is ultimately slowed by fear, we believed that typical techno-centric bravado would fail to give audiences the confidence and sense of safety to move toward a new reality. In a market crowded by opinion-leadership and bravado about the future, the landscape is ripe for a different kind of confidence—not one that shouts or provokes, or is divisive, but one that leads through serving and is empathetic, kind and inclusive.

Leveraging the content-centric marketing principles, we developed a narrative for Invitae that exemplified the company's culture, its core values, and its true form of leadership.

As with every initiative Linus engages in, we needed to craft a brand activation strategy that would guide the audience through the necessary three-part decision journey that: created 1) Recognition around a need; then encouraged 2) Exploration of the possible paths available; and then motivated the audience to undergo 3) Evaluation of the commercial options available to fulfill the need. The messaging strategy is initially internally facing language, not necessarily meant for customer consumption.

PHASE	RECOGNITION	EXPLORATION	EVALUATION
	Leadership	Education	Persuasion
MESSAGE	Through our genetics, we are all connected.	Our genetics can enable us to lead healthy lives, and we need to embrace our genetics.	Invitae is the most trusted provider of genetic testing.
NARRATIVE	Genetics is not a dividing factor but rather a common denominator that unites humanity irrespective of our cultural, racial, socio-economic, religious or political disparities. Genetically, we are more similar than different. We are all related and connected.	By embracing a genetic-filled future, we can live healthier, more fulfilling lives. Genetics unites patients with their care providers, and has the power to unite and empower families, communities, societies, and the global human community.	Invitae is the only company that makes it easy to order the right test and interpret the results, that provides counseling to communicate with patients and their families, and that makes it easy to afford so as many people as possible can be connected with their genetics.

Invitae's narrative strategy is a courageous stance, but one that is fueled by empathy for humanity and, as such, it is refreshingly different than the vast majority of Silicon Valley technology stories. This tone was a cornerstone of the Invitae brand, because it was genuine to the company's founders and the company's ethos and a timeless point of common intersection with the audience. When we realized this, we knew we had the ingredients to meet the requirements of our assignment: to provide a strong brand while allowing Invitae the nimbleness the company needed during its critical early stage.

To translate the strategy into a successful brand, we set out to accomplish two tasks. First, we needed to *enrich* Invitae's core identity beyond its functional tone and texture by extending the brand with the empathetic and organic opulence to support the company's narrative. Second, we needed to *activate* the company's brand through a Catalytic Experience that captures and demonstrates Invitae's leadership.

THE MIRACLE OF CREATIVE: ENRICHING THE BRAND

Together with the client, the Linus team decided that the core identity of Invitae could stay perfectly intact, but the company needed an extended identity to provide the necessary texture to support the message the company wanted to portray.[52] We began the brand enrichment process together with Invitae.

Starting at the Core

The company's logo mark was a beautiful and abstract depiction of a human with 23 lines depicting the chromosomes in the genome, in four subtle shades depicting the four molecules that make up the DNA 'code,' the circular shape that depicts unity, and the radiating sun-like shape that signals hope and a promise of a better tomorrow.

---

[52]A. Acker. *Building Strong Brands.* New York: Free Press, 1996.

INVITAE

Reinventing genetic testing.

FIGURE 05.02 The Invitae core identity mark, depicted with the initial tagline lockup. The company's leaders had done a magnificent job of creating this initial core identity. Just as the genome holds the answers to so many of life's questions, so did the Invitae logo provide us with so many answers for solving the company's brand activation. The Invitae logo is a trademark of the Invitae Corporation. Reproduced with permission.

©2016 Invitae—Reproduced by permission of the owner

FIGURE 05.03 Color exploration study of the Invitae logo mark revealed a textured overlay which we called 'fabric of life,' inspired by the countless ways in which the genome leads to the rich diversity in humanity.

Developing the Fabric

The Linus team leveraged the four colors within the logo to create a 'fabric' of irregular overlays to symbolize the infinite diversity that is created from the four basic building blocks of the DNA molecule.

Creating the Photo Language

To support the story of interconnectedness, we created a photographic language for Invitae that was comprised of three types of images:

1. **PORTRAITS**—Real people with their families, sometimes three or four generations of families.

2. **GENERATIONAL**—Images of people holding collections of photographs that signal ties with family history.

3. **LIFE**—Abstracts of experiences, as well as evidences of networks in nature.

Breathing Humanity into the Brand

We created a beautiful mosaic with these images to create an impressive demonstration of human diversity and our interconnectedness.

©2016 Invitae—Reproduced by permission of the owner

FIGURE 05.04 Every aspect of the Invitae brand needed to look real. Instead of relying on stock photography that so often idealizes or caricaturizes people, Invitae asked its employees, friends and families to donate an image to be built as part of the brand—a powerful internal branding effort, where the people of Invitae could quite literally see themselves in the company's brand.

we are all
connected

FIGURE 05.05 The graphic treatment of the proposed Invitae tagline shows the lockup with the four primary building blocks of life as depicted by the four solid-colored boxes, which completes the idea that we are all connected through the commonality of our DNA.

> Genetics is not a dividing factor, but rather a common denominator that unites humanity. Genetically, we are more similar than different; we are all related and we are all connected.
>
> We founded Invitae because humanity needs a new path in our genetic journey; one that further connects us as individuals, as families, and as a world.
>
> Today, we are reinventing genetic testing by lowering the barriers for clinicians and patients to obtain diagnostics and preventative genetic information. We can only do this together. Join us on this journey.

INVITAE
we are all connected

©2016 Invitae—Reproduced by permission of the owner

FIGURE 05.06 Through copy, we were able to weave Invitae's messaging of reinventing genetic testing into the first step in a much longer journey.

Writing the Tagline

It was clear that we needed to add a tagline to the company's core identity to anchor the company's leadership stance. The company's leaders fully supported our proposed tagline, which was inclusive of the company's audience as part of its identity. This was a refreshing departure from the self-centric taglines that so often dominate the business-to-business sector. The simple line 'We are all connected' became the overarching message and took the highest position of messaging hierarchy. Simple. Beautiful. Empathetic. Confident.

Connecting Tomorrow with Today

With the tagline articulating the most fundamental declaration of Invitae's philosophy and creating a timeless essence for the company, we needed to tangibly articulate its current value proposition. We made a slight modification to the company's initial headline to put it in motion and place its current efforts as one milestone along a larger journey. The simple change from "Reinventing Genetic Testing" to "Today, we are reinventing genetic testing" was the final connection we needed to make between Invitae's grand vision and its current offerings.

Engineering the Digital Presence.

As the company's most critical brand channel, we created a symphony of all brand elements through redesigning its website (Figure 05.07, pages 100–101). We carefully considered Invitae's overall user experience as another brand element and engineered an experience that mirrored the company's tone while sharing the Invitae narrative through the different parts of its home page. Our effort demonstrated Invitae's complete story—from its *Leadership* message all the way through to *Persuasion*—to a visitor in a single session.

INVITAE
FOR PATIENTS
START AN ORDER
SIGN IN
TESTING
SCIENCE
TOOLKIT
COMMUNITY
SUPPORT
ABOUT INVITAE
New paper published, a collaboration with Standford shows the clinical benefits of multi-gene hereditary cancer panels. More.
We are all connected.
GENETICS IS A COMMON DENOMINATOR THAT UNITES HUMANITY.
Our shared heritage empowers our understanding of disease, leading to more accurate diagnosis and better health.
Advancing genetic testing.
INVITAE IS A GENETIC INFORMATION COMPANY.
We are lowering the barriers to diagnostic and preventative genetic results for both clinicians and patients.
More affordable than ever before.
One price. Any test, every test.
Faster time to answers.
From sample to results within 3 weeks.
Flexible test options.
Design your own test or select a curated panel.
Deeper genetic insights.
Choose multi-gene panels or order a free re-requisition.
Confidence and quality.
Our team of gentic experts assures high-quality test results.
Explore our test catalog.
INVITAE SPECIALIZES IN GENETIC DIAGNOSTICS FOR HEREDITARY DISORDERS
Our test catalog includes disorders in a variety of medical specialties, including hereditary cancers, hematology, neurology, and pediatric genetics.

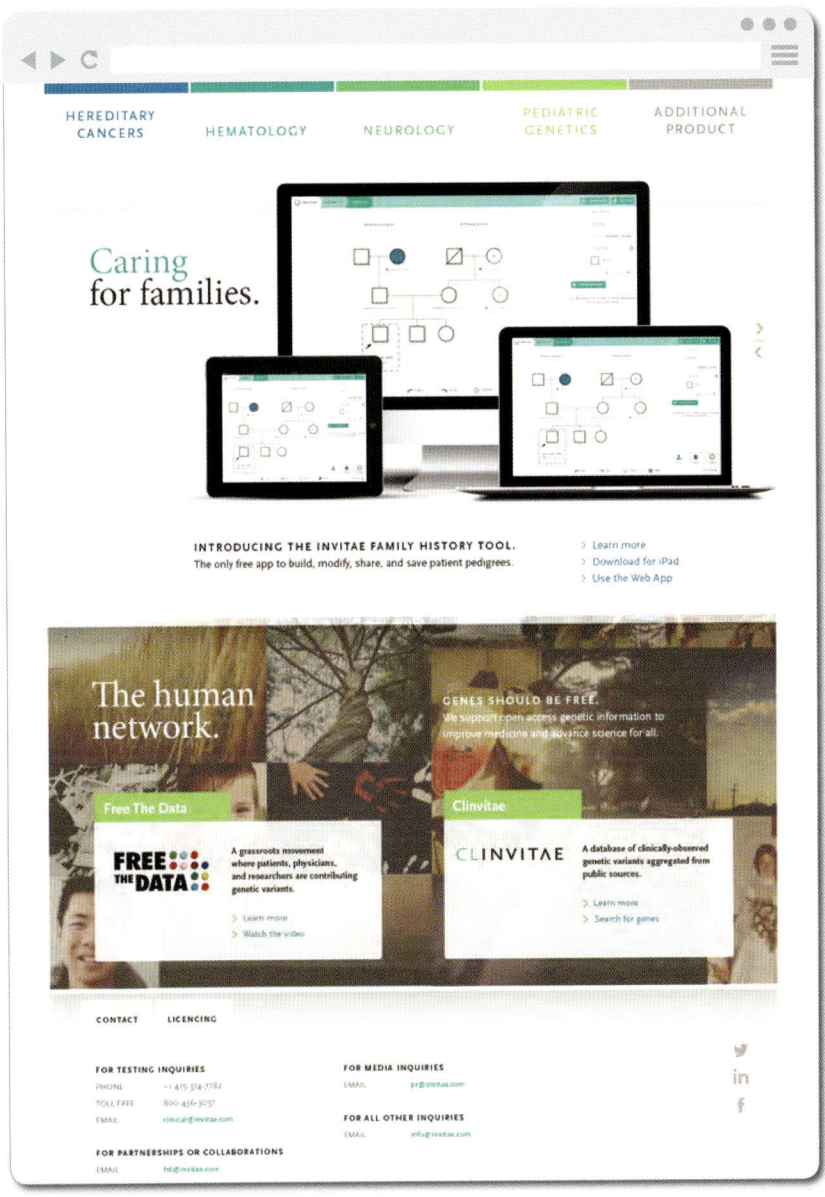

FIGURE 05.07 Invitae's new home page and website, with the full texture of the new, extended brand identity, required careful consideration of user experience, balancing content, imagery and functionality.[53]

---

[53]Invitae. "Home Page." Accessed online on April 22, 2014, at www.invitae.com.

THE CATALYTIC EXPERIENCE—
LEVERAGING STORYTELLING

Upon completion of the company's brand *enrichment*, we still needed to activate the brand through a Catalytic Experience and create an ongoing channel that enabled Invitae to demonstrate its brand promise through persistent communications.

The Catalyst

Choosing the Catalytic Experience was critical, as we needed to hit just the right balance between strength and empathy.

Recall that Myriad Genetics had lost its patent rights to the BRCA test and the strength of the company's continued service rested on the gold mine of data that it had amassed by testing thousands of patients. Invitae's core belief and a cornerstone of its vision is that people own their genetic data and should be free to do with their data as they choose. Invitae needed to raise the voice of the community to 'free the data.'

Partnering with Genetic Alliance, Invitae joined a group of other organizations to support a consortium—called Free the Data[54]—which was instrumental in the making of an extremely emotional and provocative movie (Figure 05.08). Emmy-nominated science journalist and documentary filmmaker Joanna Rudnick (who is now the creative director at Linus as of this writing but worked independently at the time) devised a brilliant plan to demonstrate Invitae's strong stance while perfectly capturing the company's kind and empathetic tone of voice.

Joanna created a perfect metaphor for how individual patients' unique data is needed to complete the full genetic picture and our understanding of genetic causes of disease. She commissioned a prominent San Francisco artist to depict the BRCA1 and BRCA2 genes in a painting. The artist created large, blank circles along the genes where individual patients had a genetic variation that

---

[54] Free the Data. "About." Accessed online on February 17, 2016, at www.free-the-data.org/about.

©2016 Invitae—Reproduced by permission of the owner

FIGURE 05.08 Still shots from the movie created by Free the Data, where director Joanna Rudnick (pictured in the fourth row, left) literally illustrates the idea that patient data will paint a clearer picture of our scientific understanding of BRCA-related cancer.[55]

---

[55]Free the Data. "Free the Data (video)." Accessed online on February 17, 2016, at youtu.be/CDZy3z0d6XE?list=PLN6y9edSAr_u9Srx7hdLRMyYtvRGo7o4s.

CATALYTIC EXPERIENCES | 103

correlated with their cancer. Each patient was invited to choose a color and paint the inside of their circle while they spoke about the importance of why they want to 'Free the Data.' The entire experience was framed as a call-to-action for patients to request their BRCA data from Myriad and share it for research purposes to increase our understanding of genetics.

When a company asserts its point of view and does so authentically with the intention of serving, it earns the honor of being seen as a leader, which is exactly the catalytic effect we intended to create in activating the brand.

The Channel

The Free the Data story enabled Invitae to enter into the global discussion about genetic testing. However, it was a single instance. Invitae also needed a way to continue demonstrating its leadership. Leveraging the beautiful stories of the patients featured in the Free the Data video as illustration of Invitae's connection with its audiences, we created a Patient Stories channel with Invitae, where we featured the brave and emotional journeys of selected patients.

This channel became a cornerstone of Invitae's social media strategy, where patients share their stories in any form. A short perusal of Invitae's Facebook page will leave an impression that we are all connected.

As we completed our work, the head of marketing at Invitae complimented us for the work we had created by saying, "We now have a brand that we can grow into!"

THE OUTCOME

It is often difficult to isolate the effect of a brand on the company's performance. I firmly believe that to ask about a brand's Return on Investment (ROI) in science and healthcare is to ask the wrong question.

Even in today's 'measure-everything-track-everyone' digital landscape, there are still no direct measures of brand performance unless all other variables are held constant. While in some mature consumer goods markets it is possible to isolate the effectiveness of branding, faster-paced business-to-business environments rarely allow for this level of isolated measurement.

A company's brand is among the three most important assets of the company and on par with mission and strategy. We do not attempt to isolate the performance of a company's mission, and neither should we ask the same of its brand. Instead, the company's total performance is the full measure of all three facets of the entity, which are intimately interconnected and linked to one another.

A few months after Invitae articulated and activated its updated brand, mission and strategy, it orchestrated a highly successful Initial Public Offering in February 2015, raising over $100M.[56] The company has steadily continued expanding its testing menu and its reach. In 2015, Invitae grew the number of genetic test reports it delivered by 5000% to over 19,000 patients,[57] and the company plans to continue the rapid growth in years to come.

With a singular focus on its mission to "bring comprehensive genetic information into mainstream medical practice to improve the quality of healthcare for billions of people,"[58] Invitae is determined to create the world they wish for themselves and all of humanity. And having had the privilege to collaborate with the Invitae's senior leadership, I cannot think of a greater group of people I would trust to usher us toward our genetic future.

---

[56] Nasdaq. "INVITAE CORP (NVTA) IPO." Accessed online on February 17, 2016, at www.nasdaq.com/markets/ipos/company/invitae-corp-837176-77421.

[57] Invitae. "Invitae announces full year 2015 financial results and 2016 business objectives." Accessed online on February 17, 2016, at www.invitae.com/en/press/invitae-full-year-2015-financial-2016-business-objectives/.

[58] Nasdaq. "INVITAE CORP (NVTA) IPO." Accessed online on February 17, 2016, at www.nasdaq.com/markets/ipos/company/invitae-corp-837176-77421.

CHAPTER 6

Passion in Science

New England Biolabs

Solidifying a Company's Connection to New Audiences

SYNOPSIS

How does a company transfer the goodwill and relationships it has built with an audience in order to diversify the range of that audience—despite rapid changes in technology, the industry and communications—all while staying true to itself?

This is a story about a successful company that has, for 40 years, navigated the changing world with strength and integrity, evolving as technology has advanced, watching companies come and go, engaging in the succession of its founder as CEO and competing in different industrial landscapes. In order to continue its success, New England Biolabs (NEB) wanted to secure its foundation and build a meaningful relationship with a wider range of scientists, including the newer generation. This posed a difficult dilemma, since certain audience segments, such as 'digital natives,' build relationships with companies differently than others.

In this chapter, I will discuss the following:

- Moving beyond mere products to form a relationship with a wider range of scientists
- Leveraging the Content-Centric Model to build a new class of thought-leadership
- Developing a new communications modality without risking existing relationships with loyal customers

- Developing a campaign that *demonstrates* values as opposed to just *saying* them
- Humanizing a brand
- Creating an experiential marketing campaign and leveraging it beyond the experience itself

The NEB story shows best practices for how a company moves from talking about what it does to *why* it does it. In this case, NEB took a bold step toward this as a way of celebrating its age, without getting old.

TRUE VALUE

You do not have to know much about New England Biolabs to immediately *feel* the special quality that the company exudes the first time you interact with it. Whether you are a customer of its wide breadth of products used for life science research, a company who sources its products as an ingredient (also referred to as OEM) for your own solutions, an employee, or even a consultant, any interaction with NEB is starkly different than what you will experience in today's techno-centric business world.

A part of me felt disbelief that a company in today's industry can sustain itself with such aspirations to be its best self, not cutting a single corner or creating compromises in its product quality, its level of service or its commitment to what it believes to be the right thing to do. To say that NEB has sustained itself in the changing landscape for over 40 years would not grant adequate credit to the company. It has thrived!

In the spectrum of the life sciences, NEB is a medium-sized, independent company. Throughout its history, NEB has steadfastly remained committed to its way while mergers and acquisitions have built relatively behemoth companies with much larger distribution capabilities and strategies. Yet NEB continues to thrive, and its customers love the company. This love has been built through the company's entire history. NEB has made a positive, deep-rooted brand impression slowly, over time, with consistent actions.

With this campaign, we aimed to communicate NEB's values as the basis of the company's relationship with the world, so that current and future generations of scientists would appreciate the company beyond its product portfolio. Would NEB need to change the way it builds relationships? And would this change be genuine to its values? The current generation of up-and-coming scientists is digitally-connected. These scientists enjoy their independence. They are empowered by their ability to bypass the practice of scientific apprenticeship. They may not have experienced the full depth of how NEB views its relationships with customers. As with my own experience with NEB, some may not even know that a company such as NEB can even exist in science.

On the eve of NEB's 40th anniversary, as mergers and acquisitions continued to dominate the life science industry and the younger generation of scientists continued to enter the workforce, we wondered if NEB would become dwarfed by these powerful conglomerates, who had the muscle and the digital capability to squeeze out 'the little guy' and reach a wide range of scientists to win their share-of-wallet.

It was this question my team and I were invited to collaborate with NEB to answer. The Linus Group and NEB worked hand-in-hand in a rare collaboration that blurred the boundaries between our team and theirs to become a single unit. In this story, my reference to 'the team' signifies this close collaboration between NEB and The Linus Group. We worked together to tell the company story and implement a campaign that creates awareness about NEB to solidify its brand beyond its products and strengthen its footprint based on its values and impact rather than its company size.

SITUATION ANALYSIS: THREE SIDES OF THE TRUTH

Company Dynamics—The Company's Side of the Truth

New England Biolabs has amassed a large catalog of many hundreds of recombinant enzymes that are critical for a wide variety of techniques for molecular biology or, more specifically, what the executive director of research refers to as "the scissors, the copy machines, the glue and the shredders" that enable basic manipulation of the DNA molecule.[59]

In 1975, a group of scientists got together under the leadership of Don Comb to form NEB, just as modern molecular biology approaches were being discovered, with the idea of providing commercial-grade products. From the start, the foundation of New England Biolabs' success was its product catalog, which housed a rich library of scientific primers, visual explanations of the scientific processes, protocol information and other technical content. Soon, the NEB catalog became heralded in academia and industry as a true and valuable resource and the cornerstone of why scientists view NEB with tremendous affection. For nearly 40 years, NEB leveraged best practices in content marketing to win brand loyalty.

Researchers still covet the NEB catalog. In the past decade, however, as more researchers find information online, NEB has made great measures to translate its catalog and its content to the digital world. Dealing with the digital currency of the attention economy has not been easy for NEB, as it has not been easy for the majority of life science suppliers.

Today, every company dazzles scientists with impressive product portfolios and numerous technical resources. Though NEB was the early leader of this technique, its strategy has become a parity play, and we determined early in our collaboration that the key to NEB's success needed to be about more than its products.

Every product has a natural life cycle. Every strategy exhausts its effectiveness at some point. Markets change. Even people within a company come and go. And yet some aspects of a company must remain solid, intact and timeless. Without that essence, the company is more susceptible to falling prey to change, losing its way and its ability to fulfill its true destiny. It may be articulated in a mission, a vision, or a set of core values, or some other document, or it may be experienced without words.

---

[59]New England Biolabs. "About NEB." Accessed online on February 22, 2016, at www.neb.com/about-neb.

Most companies have a mission and vision statement. Some have core values. Very few actually live by any of these tenets. Perhaps companies and leaders conclude that there is no substantive room for such lofty (and, frankly, often meaningless) corporate-speak in the exciting technical rigor of 'the work' that drives their employees and customers. Perhaps it is due to the 'short-termism' that has taken over the global business landscape, with the rise of finance as the main instrument for making money, where businesses build and run more often with a near-term exit strategy. Irrespective of the reason, few companies have a truly unique and well-defined culture.

New England Biolabs is amongst these few. Though they have never formally defined it with words, this company has created the world in which its leadership wants to live, work and contribute. Joanna Rudnick, Linus' creative director, and I spent a week at the NEB campus to try to understand how to capture and articulate the company's message. As we immersed ourselves within the company's daily activities and held conversations with the team, a core, timeless truth of the company clearly emerged:

Empathy.

Empathy is the fuel on which New England Biolabs runs. It fuels the company's passion. It drives NEB to focus on improving the world, beyond creating excellent products and providing good service. And it provides the basis of its culture. Empathy runs deep at NEB. There are manifestations of this level of empathy everywhere, and with everyone, at NEB. As the collective team spent the week together, we started to notice a pattern of four distinct pillars where the company's ethos of empathy fuels the company's values:

- **PASSION FOR SCIENTIFIC EXCELLENCE**—Founded by Donald Comb, New England Biolabs is largely made up of scientists who care for, and are passionate about, advancing science. Their culture and passion for science permeates the organization. They care deeply about science, and their entire company is built around pushing forward, including their own basic research initiatives.

- **PASSION FOR HUMANITY**—Although it takes great pride in enabling the advancement of science through its products and services, it is not merely enough for New England Biolabs to feel it has done everything it can. The aforementioned basic research program at NEB includes a focus on understanding and improving some of the most neglected conditions that affect the most underprivileged people on earth that are underfunded within the global research community. NEB spends a relatively large portion of its income to advance humanity.

- **PASSION FOR THE ENVIRONMENT**—From ensuring that the company minimizes its use of energy through a LEED-certified facility, to a chemical-free water treatment facility that returns the company's waste water to the environment in a more pure state than the water it receives, to its founding of an initiative to create a "genome bank dedicated to exploring and preserving the threatened biological diversity of the sea,"[60] it is no surprise that NEB was the first company to start a Styrofoam packaging return and recycling program for the shipping containers of its products.

- **PASSION FOR CREATIVITY**—The company believes that creativity is the spark for all advancement in humanity. It is through creativity that we connect with one another, imagine new possibilities, and solve the world's greatest challenges. NEB actively encourages creativity through its support of the arts to spur new kinds of ideas, conversations and approaches within its team.

While many companies take credit for serving science or pushing science forward, New England Biolabs' employees live it every day. And they do it not to maximize profits, but simply because they care.

This rich alchemy of the company's values translates to its products and services. It is the 'why' behind the company's existence. We wanted to capture this story and tell the world. How would we tell such a story about this amazing company without cheapening the authenticity and the purity of NEB's true intentions? But the bigger question that plagued us was whether the diverse set of scientists would even care, given the massive growth of competitors.

---

[60]Northeastern University. "The Ocean Genome Legacy Center of New England Biolabs." Accessed online on February 22, 2016, at www.northeastern.edu/cos/marinescience/ogl/.

Competitive Dynamics—The Market's Side of the Truth

As I mentioned previously, the market around New England Biolabs was full of mergers and acquisitions, creating new classes of companies that vie to outfit entire laboratories with every piece of equipment and complete workflows for scientific protocols and methods. These large companies have more massive distribution capabilities, becoming preferred providers to academic institutions, as well as industry in an attempt to maximize their customers' share-of-wallet and locking out the smaller, boutique providers of niche products and services.

One by one, companies small and large have started neutralizing NEB's subtle differentiators, amassing large portfolios of molecular biology products, touting quality and superior service, offering educational resources, and even taking back Styrofoam shipping boxes.

To a scientist with no historical appreciation or brand preferences, the landscape looks like a sea of sameness. It is no wonder that this scientist would choose the lowest price, the most convenient distribution channel, or the brand that makes him/her laugh for a second on Facebook.

Customer Dynamics—The Customer's Side of the Truth

In talking with the company's target audience through in-depth telephone interviews, we quickly validated the positive association that experienced scientists displayed toward NEB. We divided the groups into seasoned scientists, who were current customers, and newer scientists. Statements about NEB from the seasoned scientists contained intimate words such as *love*, *care*, *good* and *kindred*. When asked to connect these feelings with stories, audiences would almost invariably tell of their first experience with the company, either describing the utility they had received from the NEB catalog or an above-and-beyond level of customer care that the company had provided them. These associations were still as vivid and as solid as their first encounter for the more experienced scientists. This was starkly contrasted by slightly negative associations the same scientists felt toward the large conglomerate companies, expressing a resistance against the notion of hegemony or dominance by any one company.

The newer generation, on the other hand, were apathetic about the commercial landscape in general. They did not know about NEB's rich history (a few referred to the company as a startup). They displayed a general air of skepticism about corporate entities and they had a preconceived notion about corporate agendas.

Then the conversations turned toward Facebook. The social media platform can be seen as a microcosm for the human condition and group behavior.[61] Though actual experimentation has caused concern and controversy,[62] Facebook is now part of our society's fabric and arguably shapes our feelings and behavior through psychological phenomena such as emotional contagion.[63] What interested us, however, was to learn how the diverse audience—especially young scientists—connected with the digital world. More specifically, why do people spend time on social media sites such as Twitter or Facebook? Why do we spend hours every day looking and scrolling backward in time? What are we looking for?

It is easy to slide into a cynical perspective about the effect of social media, riddled with opinions and points of view and snarky comments about others through the bravado of anonymity or righteousness. And it is easy to get sucked into sensationalism, scandal and social phenomena, as we are bombarded with such content every day. But is that truly what we seek in our hours of endless scrolls on Facebook?

I have far more faith in humanity than this cynical view. I believe that with our increasing physical disconnection with our communities, we seek authenticity in the digital realm. This was evidenced in our conversations with the additional scientist audiences as well, and we posited that what they truly seek is realness, and they judge it through stories, demonstration or action: a friend's epic journey to the top of Mt. Kilimanjaro to celebrate her 40th birthday is uplifting and inspiring; a professor's TED talk about the perseverance required to travel through the uncharted waters of scientific discovery strikes a true chord;

---

[61] M. Kosinski. "Will Facebook Replace Traditional Research Methods?" Insights by *Stanford Business*, October 8, 2015. Accessed online on February 23, 2016, at www.gsb.stanford.edu/insights/will-facebook-replace-traditional-research-methods.

[62] K. Waldman. "Facebook's Unethical Experiment" *Slate*, June 28, 2014. Accessed online on February 23, 2016, at www.slate.com/articles/health_and_science/science/2014/06/facebook_unethical_experiment_it_made_news_feeds_happier_or_sadder_to_manipulate.html.

[63] A D. I. Kramera, J.E. Guillory J. T. Hancock. "Experimental evidence of massive-scale emotional contagion through social networks." *PNAS*, June 17, 2014. Vol. 111, no. 24, at www.pnas.org/content/111/24/8788.

a company's humorous video that demonstrates that they are empathetic grabs attention; and perhaps the most profound idea as to why we consume, 'like' and share the experiences that move us in this increasingly virtual society is because they provide an avenue for us to authenticate ourselves.

This realization and philosophy resonated with us, as well as with the culture and philosophy of NEB. By seeking all three sides of the truth, we had arrived at an interesting intersection, and an un-ignorable insight.

The Full Story

Our synthesis about the full story rested on the intangible, emotional side of the spectrum.

> Scientists are moved by authentic experiences that match their ideals.

As you have undoubtedly surmised, this strategy was not going to be about NEB's enzymes or kits. It was not going to attempt to relive the past or take credit for the company's pioneering ways. It was about resonating with audiences, and serving a deep, emotional need that they crave—that everyone craves: a chance to feel, authentically.

CREATING THE BACKBONE OF THE STORY

Positioning NEB

Again, while the formal positioning construct is typically used to articulate the strategy of products or technologies, I see it as an exercise in rigor to articulate the core of a company's positioning, irrespective of the offering. The positioning statement for NEB reads as follows:

Formal Positioning Statement

> *For* current and future generations of scientists
>
> *Who need* to be empowered to make decisions that match their own sense of values

New England Biolabs

Provides a company that believes values are the timeless essence of an organization

Unlike other companies that are primarily driven by money, technology and/or providing one-stop-shops for scientists,

Only NEB dedicates itself to manifesting its beliefs through each and every interaction with its customers.

Admittedly, claiming superiority over other companies in order to create differentiation was difficult for us, given NEB's culture of inclusivity, respect and honor for others. The final statement that describes the competition in the 'unlike' portion of the positioning statement may overly celebrate the direction of the other companies in the industry.

We also distilled the essence of value that NEB provides in a value proposition statement for the purpose of aligning internal groups.[64]

Value Proposition

New England Biolabs cares passionately about science, the creative arts, the betterment of humanity and the protection of the environment.

It was now time to create a richer narrative to match the scientific decision journey.

BUILDING THE STORY: THE CONTENT-CENTRIC MESSAGING STRATEGY

Leveraging the Content-Centric Marketing Model, the narrative for New England Biolabs was the perfect overlay of a common truth that the company and its audiences shared.

As mentioned earlier, the messaging strategy is initially internally facing language and not necessarily meant for customer consumption. As the team

---

[64] Positioning and value proposition statements are internal strategy documents, not audience-facing messaging.

PHASE	RECOGNITION	EXPLORATION	EVALUATION
	Leadership	Education	Persuasion
MESSAGE	Values are timeless.	Scientists are driven by their own values.	New England Biolabs cares passionately about science, creativity, the betterment of humanity and the protection of the environment.
NARRATIVE	In the world of rapidly changing technology, business modalities and communications, scientists want to feel that their own values are authentic, so that they can rely on them to navigate change.	Scientists are more empowered than ever to find information and to make things happen on their own, guided by their own passions and their ideals. They engage with those with whom they share common values.	Every aspect of NEB's business is guided by a passion for science, humanity, the environment and creativity, which are evident in every interaction with every customer.

came to consensus about the positioning statement, Joanna and I exchanged a glance, knowing that we had our work cut out for us.

A narrative, such as the one above, cannot be uttered by any company wishing to maintain credibility. Instead, it needs to be fully experienced. The crux of this assignment was still ahead of us—to create a campaign architecture that communicates the message above without saying it.

THE MIRACLE OF CREATIVE: ENRICHING THE BRAND

"The devil is in the details," the common saying goes. Beginning the creative process by developing a campaign architecture ensures that all of the details are addressed, and each phase of the campaign tackles any specific issues or barriers to success. This work happens hand-in-hand with the creative development.

The creative team at Linus, in collaboration with NEB, needed to devise a program that clearly defined the four necessary value pillars without the slightest hint of boastfulness or self-righteousness that would be detrimental to NEB's authentic voice: How do we humanize the NEB brand?

How would NEB act as a person? How would they view the world? How would they interact with their community? In these questions, we realized the answer:

NEB would never tout its own values. Instead, they would celebrate others in the community who display such values instead!

Hence, the New England Biolabs' Passion in Science Awards™ was born. We leveraged the company's upcoming 40th anniversary as the impetus to launch

PHASE	RECOGNITION	EXPLORATION	EVALUATION
INVOKING	CREATIVITY	HYPOTHESIS	VALIDATION
	Leadership	Education	Persuasion
MESSAGE	Values are timeless.	Scientists are driven by their values.	New England Biolabs cares passionately about science, creativity, the betterment of humanity and the protection of the environment.
OBJECTIVES	Reframe the conversation and introduce another aspect of purchasing that most scientists may not consider in their technical everyday realities: values.	Demonstrate how scientists are driven by their own values and how their own personal passion plays a significant role in their science and careers.	Create a core common truth between scientists and NEB.
BARRIERS	The expected norm of corporate communications is about products. Though this is an opportunity to differentiate, this kind of communication must be handled with care.	Scientists need first to see their peers making decisions based on values before they are willing to accept the values of a company as a proxy for their own.	NEB cannot overplay its values, lest it lose its authenticity among its loyal core followers and may be seen as 'selling out.'
STRATEGY	Orchestrate an experience that creates desire for scientists to ponder the importance of values in science.	Encourage scientists to inventory their own demonstration of values or those of colleagues and their scientific community.	By celebrating and capturing the demonstration of values in others, assert the overlap between NEB's own values and those of the award winners.
SOLUTION	Announce an award program for scientists who have taken action to demonstrate one of four values: excellence in science, care for humanity, environmental stewardship and creativity in science.	A call for entries where scientists can nominate themselves or colleagues to win an award based on their actions to demonstrate leadership in one of four values: science, humanity, environment and creativity.	Host an award ceremony event that brings the diverse group of winners together to discuss their stories and share ideas about the future. Create a documentary-style film of the event for distribution.

CATALYTIC EXPERIENCES | 119

this award, where scientists could apply or nominate others who have incorporated one of the four values into their science and their scientific careers. Each of the four prize categories aligned with each of the four value pillars, encouraging the community to engage with detailed explanations for why each pillar is a necessary value for advancing science in a responsible way.

The overall campaign architecture is summarized in the table on the previous page, articulating the objective, the barrier, strategy, and specific solution for each stage of the campaign.

THE CATALYTIC EXPERIENCE—LEVERAGING STORYTELLING

The story in this campaign would unfold in real time, as NEB announced the awards and solicited entries, selected the winners and celebrated them through a two-day event at the company's main campus in Ipswich, Massachusetts. The team created a documentary about the event and celebrated the winners of each award category.

1. LEADERSHIP

Developing a series of advertisements, NEB leveraged its own social media channels as well as paid advertisement through several scientific social media channels (e.g., *The Scientist*) to reach audiences. The company specifically chose social channels to reach the next generation of younger audiences and supplemented internal lists to include its own customer base and followers.

2. EDUCATION

Together with the team at NEB and the help of software service provider Skild,[65] we developed an award-submission platform to describe, educate, solicit and capture award application submissions, and a full back-end system for the NEB to manage submissions and select winners.

---

[65]Skild. "Home Page." Accessible via http://www.skild.com.

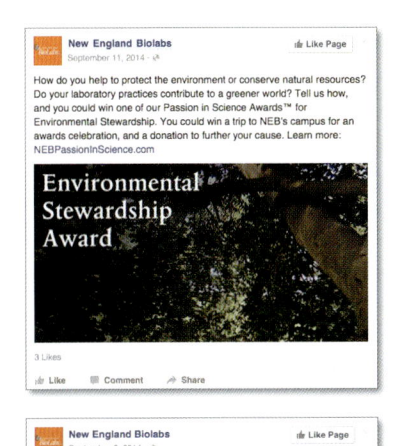

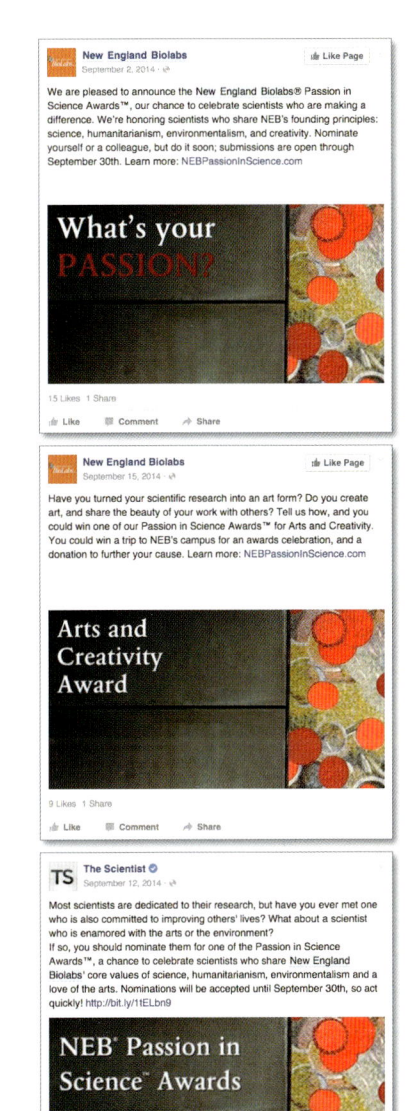

FIGURE 06.01 The series of advertisements created to feature the Passion in Science awards ceremony, as well as for the specific value pillars, was circulated through Facebook[66]

[66]New England Biolabs. "Advertisement series." Accessed online via Facebook on September 18, 2016, at www.facebook.com.

CATALYTIC EXPERIENCES | 121

It was critical to capture the perfect tone for the award submissions website. The site needed to clearly justify NEB's interest in the awards and each value pillar, while inspiring scientists to consider how these values manifest in their own science and careers.

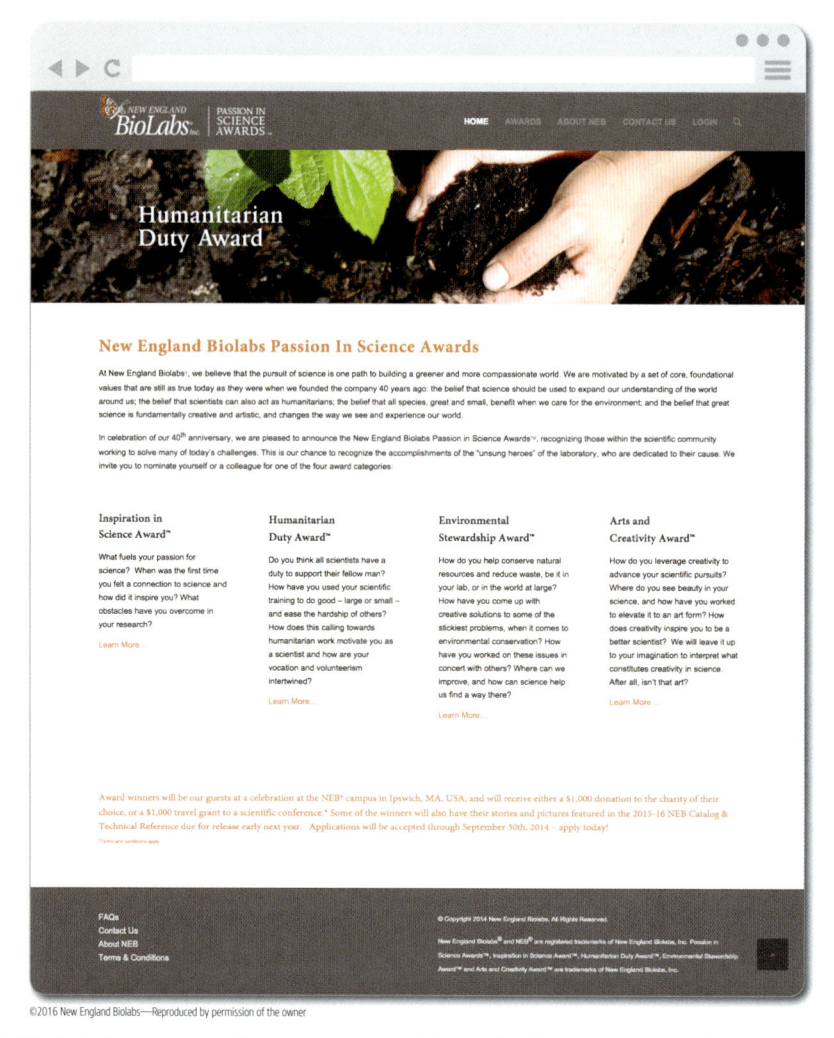

FIGURE 06.02 The home page of the award submission website describes the awards, supporting the Leadership message and delivering the importance of values in science. The tone was sincere when describing NEB's intention, but inspirational for the scientist.[67]

[67]Reprinted from nebpassioninscience.com (2014) with permission from New England Biolabs.

3. PERSUASION

On a fresh autumn morning in 2014, fifteen scientists arrived at New England Biolabs' beautiful campus in Ipswich, Massachusetts, for a two-day event to share their stories, learn from one another and from their hosts, grow together, and celebrate the dedication of their work in exemplifying each of the four value pillars. The entire event was captured on video through Joanna Rudnick's direction (Figure 06.03, page 124). The result was a documentary of fifteen amazing people celebrated by a company that truly sees them and celebrates their dedication in navigating their science and careers based on timeless values that matter.

THE OUTCOME

One month after the event, I emailed Jim Ellard, the CEO of New England Biolabs, to see how he felt about the event. My phone rang two minutes later. Instead of replying to my email, he said he thought it better to call. After exchanging quick updates on each other's lives and families, Jim expressed to me how transformative he felt the awards ceremony was and how successful he found the endeavor, even prior to the final publication of the movie.

Clearly this campaign was about much more than a mere marketing tactic for NEB. The process and the event seemed to have had more profound effects on the company internally as well as the market.

NEB received over 140 applications for awards, and the documentary is available on the NEB site for viewing, as a constant reminder to the world that there is so much more than meets the eye than NEB's fantastic products and superb service.

The company also leveraged this campaign to reaffirm its values to the market, but the experience had positive internal effects, galvanizing and energizing the company's employees as they felt celebrated and part of a much more noble cause and a worthy mission. NEB included profiles of the award winners in its much-revered annual catalog.

©2016 New England Biolabs—Reproduced by permission of the owner

FIGURE 06.03 Still images from the documentary of the NEB Passion in Science 2014 awards ceremony, depicting the rich diversity in thinking, creativity and passion that NEB brought together by orchestrating such an event.[68]

---

[68]New England Biolabs. "2014 NEB Passion in Science Awards (video)." Accessed online via YouTube on February 23, 2016, at youtu.be/SIfffl3mVa8.

FIGURE 06.04 An excerpt of NEB's 2015 catalog illustrates how the company leveraged the stories and work of its award winners to demonstrate its own value to audiences.[69]

This award ceremony also became the precursor for the company to adopt a new corporate tagline that perfectly finds the core common truth that NEB hopes to share with its customers, collaborators and partners: *Be Inspired. Drive Discovery. Stay Genuine*.

NEB is driven by a unique passion for operating the company based on its values. This campaign articulated NEB's values for the first time and aimed to elevate the company's value proposition beyond its product portfolio. If a company's values are genuine, they do not change with the times, and they are always a point of common ground between the company and its public. NEB's values will resonate with future generations of scientists just as authentically as they have for the past 40 years.

---

[69]The New England Biolabs Catalog can be accessed online at www.neb.com.

CATALYTIC EXPERIENCES | 125

CHAPTER 7

A Better Tip

Biotix

Creating a Digital Infrastructure to Drive the Audience's Decision Journey

SYNOPSIS

The vast majority of the industry agrees that engaging content is the most critical factor for successful digital marketing. Whether the end goal is to generate leads or change perceptions about a product or a brand, the main challenge that marketers face is effective coordination between outbound efforts and inbound channels to create a seamless experience for audiences and usher them toward a positive decision. The key to successful digital marketing is to engineer the audience's experience based on their natural decision-making journey, and nowhere is the Content-Centric Marketing Model more salient then in the development of a digital property. By following the three phases of a scientist or clinician's decision-making journey, marketers should develop appropriate content and architect a user experience that naturally leads them to the intended goal.

In this chapter, I illustrate the story of Biotix, a scientific consumables company that had all the makings of a successful marketing campaign: a strong offering, a unique point of view, and the courage to break tradition. What it was missing was the digital infrastructure and the right tone of voice to generate significant interest. Let us discover how Biotix developed a strong digital presence and generated awareness on a massive scale in a short period of time.

Throughout this story, I explore the following concepts:
- Assessing the landscape through 'The Four Ps of Marketing'
- Applying the Content-Centric Marketing Model to a consumable product line
- Using the scientist's decision journey to architect a digital user experience
- Leveraging social media as the main outbound channel to generate tremendous awareness

The confidence that Biotix's leaders displayed was a major underlying ingredient for their success in generating awareness on social media. However, their boldness was nested with careful planning and diligent validation to ensure a positive outcome.

ONE HOT TIP

Most scientific experiments at some point involve moving a precise amount of liquid from one vessel to another. Whether taking a small amount of a sample for analysis or mixing or adding reagents to perform a reaction, liquid handling is a major part of how science gets done.

The vast majority of scientific liquids pass through a pipette tip—a small, usually plastic vessel—that fits at the end of a pipette and extracts a sample of liquid from a container and dispenses it elsewhere. Commonly employed as a single-use consumable, it is little wonder why the huge pipette tip market is under tremendous competition from well-known premium brands to virtually unbranded commodity offerings.

Given the lack of scientific or application-level positioning and relatively incremental product improvements to differentiate offerings, brand loyalty is the name of the game in the pipette tip market. Unless they experience a failure, scientists and laboratory workers have little reason to switch their pipette tip brands.

Pipette

Pipette Tip

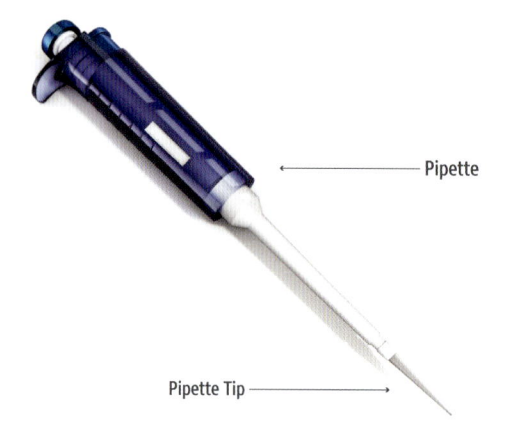

FIGURE 07.01 A 3D rendering of a manual pipette with the disposable tip attached.[70]

Compared to the top competitors, most of whom sell pipettes and tips alongside a large portfolio of other labware offerings, Biotix is a small and relatively new entrant on the scene. Powered by the creativity and work of a passionate engineer who founded the brand and a seasoned executive with astute sensibilities, Biotix designed and manufactured a superior pipette tip, receiving five patents for its novel design. However, Biotix was fighting a large, uphill battle in gaining mainstream adoption due to low brand awareness.

While sales have grown steadily year-over-year for Biotix brand tips since launch, by 2015 the company's share of the overall pipette tip market was still in the low single-digits. Given this considerable headroom for growth, Biotix wanted to maximize its exposure to gain mass brand awareness for what it believed was an advanced pipette tip.

The question was how.

Cutting through the noise of a crowded, price-sensitive market in a product category that few scientists care about and have little desire to change would require an unconventional marketing strategy. Luckily, the leadership at Biotix was just as open to breaking convention with their brand as they were intent on

[70]Image Copyright: dny3d / 123RF Stock Photo.

breaking convention with their product. We needed to ensure that we leveraged their desire to be bold with great care, so we dove into our situation analysis process with a keen eye toward finding an actionable insight that would allow us to find a core common truth between Biotix and the market.

SITUATION ANALYSIS: THREE SIDES OF THE TRUTH

Company Dynamics—The Company's Side of the Truth

A company's marketing strategy has four facets, articulated through an alliteration: *Product, Place, Price and Promotion.*[71] Often referred to as the 'The Marketing Mix' or 'The Four Ps of Marketing,' this simple and effective model is a powerful underlying basis of all marketing strategies. Creating a winning marketing strategy requires the manager to apply smart and creative thinking to each of these four levers to develop a winning strategy.

With such a convoluted market, the Marketing Mix proved the best way to gain a clear understanding of Biotix's strategy and the competitive landscape. We first analyzed Biotix:

Product

What happens when you completely rethink and redesign a small, commodity component of a system? The founder and current Chief Technology Officer of Biotix has devoted his career to pursuit of the most optimum pipette tip in the world, resulting in five new patents for the Biotix brand products. These five new features translated into benefits in increased accuracy and precision by removing some user dependencies through better engineering, improving ergonomics by requiring less force to attach and detach a tip to and from a pipette and enhancing pipetting hygiene by adding an indicator dye that alerts the user of the possibility of contamination of their pipette due to too much suction.

---

[71]"Marketing Mix." Wikipedia. Accessed online on April 7, 2016, at en.wikipedia.org/wiki/Marketing_mix.

Place

Within the science and medical industries, in markets that require complex sales processes and have few point-of-sale opportunities with customers, the long-standing Place strategy has been limited to the use of aggregators called distributors, who create exhaustive product portfolios and develop the sales, shipping and logistical management of purchasing for companies. In the sciences, there are two global distributors—VWR and Fisher Scientific—who collectively process more than half of the volume of transactions made through distributors and compete fiercely with each other to gain accounts. Given the experience of its senior leadership, Biotix developed a strong relationship with VWR to handle all of the sales logistics.

Price

Mapping all of the pipette tips from the industry across the price/performance spectrum, three rough clusters appear: low-end commodity tips, midrange tips and premium tips. With superior performance, the team priced the Biotix tips in the lower end of the premium tips spectrum, demonstrating significant value for the price.

Promotion

Understanding the dynamics within distributors, Biotix needed to not only drive interest for its products, but it also needed to incentivize the distributors' own sales reps to proactively offer the Biotix tips to their customers. Biotix crafted a series of attractive promotions through its distributor relationships and developed a traditional marketing communications presence in an attempt to create brand awareness directly with scientists in order to generate 'pull' for the company's brand.

Biotix positioned its brand with the tagline "A better tip" to signal its improved performance, ergonomics and hygiene through its five differentiating features—a functional message that was pushed through a modest outbound advertising and direct email campaign.

At the start, the Biotix website offered a digital brochure with videos, a product list and a few calls-to-action. Due to the complexity of the company's relationships with distributors, it had not engineered a path to advance the scientist's own decision-journey all the way to purchase, and any leads generated would be manually processed and sent to the appropriate distributor in hopes of follow-up.

After several years of growth, the company's leadership agreed it was time to accelerate progress for their Biotix brand tips. With relatively few new products in the pipeline and an outsourced sales strategy with distributors, the leadership saw marketing as the practical mechanism for organic growth acceleration.

Competitive Dynamics—The Market's Side of the Truth

While the pipette tip market is saturated with offerings across the price/performance spectrum, we noticed several patterns emerging when we surveyed the competitive landscape through the lens of the Four Ps of Marketing:

Product

Virtually every company discusses performance (accuracy and precision). As a result, the terms became table-stakes for the product category and turned into generalized noise in a sea of sameness. Since the actual accuracy and precision of pipetting is user-dependent, most companies provide guidelines for good pipetting techniques.

Some companies use ergonomic and usability benefits to position their offerings, but most of these companies largely attribute ergonomics and usability to the pipette itself, which is the physical product held in the user's hand. In such cases, tips are sold as part of a 'system' without specific value propositions of their own.

We found that no other company positioned its tips around the concept of hygiene. Many mention their sterilization options and the inert nature of their polymer blends, but these statements are typically mentioned almost as an afterthought.

Place

The competitive dynamics within the industry mostly revolve around channel strategies regarding distributors, and three common strategies dominate the channel strategies:

- **DISCOUNTING**—Distributors earn their fees by receiving the goods from a manufacturer at a discount. Therefore it is typically to the distributor's advantage to push products from manufacturers from which they have the deepest discounts.
- **BRAND EXCLUSIVITY**—Companies with coveted brands agree to distribute them exclusively or through a select number of distributors so as to provide a differentiator to that distributor in the eyes of the end customer in exchange for the lowest dealer discount or the highest volume and visibility within the distributor's offerings.
- **PRIVATE-LABELING**—Some manufacturers offer to take their own brand name off their products and just sell their products under the brand name of the distributor itself in exchange for higher volume sales or guaranteed sales.

Price

As with many consumables or goods, brands often use price to signal a premium offering or to entice higher-volume sales. We found that the competitive landscape in the pipette category followed this convention without any interesting or differentiating pricing strategies.

Promotion

Often, companies in the laboratory products and consumables industry offer promotions directly or through distributors. The companies frequently offer promotions to tempt users to change brands. Those who have broad portfolios typically bundle their pipette tips with pipettes or other products in order to entice users to experience their pipette tips. Others try discounts or other promotional giveaways to first-time customers. Researchers have long examined the short- and long-term effectiveness of pricing promotions and discounts, so it is unclear as to whether the companies that employ promotions for laboratory products are actually gaining long-term profitable business growth. Regardless of their effect, we did not uncover any unique or differentiating promotional strategies beyond the routine and expected discounts and premium bundling in the pipette tip category.

Given this tour of the market landscape, it became exceedingly clear that everyone—including Biotix—talked about the same benefits, employed the same channels and offered the same promotions. To find a winning strategy to differentiate Biotix, we needed to examine the third side of the truth: the voice of customers.

Customer Dynamics—The Customer's Side of Truth

As part of our standard practice in developing sound marketing strategies, we surveyed a sampling of scientists and also selected a cohort of scientists who represent the target customers to engage in in-depth interviews. We validated our hypotheses and gained nuanced information from this qualitative work.

It should be noted that most scientists do not overtly think about their pipette tips at all. Most say they have their favorite brands, either because they use the same brand of tips as their pipette or due to non-functional personal preference. Most say they choose pipettes based on price. Scientists know many companies covet their loyalty and business.

Given the crowded and hyper-aggressive nature of this market, customers feel inundated with marketing and promotions for pipettes and tips. Most just turn a blind eye to it as they have little reason to switch from their current brand. The more experienced scientists with whom we spoke seemed loyal to their preferred brands while the younger scientists saw tips as commodities and seemed too cool to care about such an 'insignificant' aspect of their laboratory work.

They all hear messages about ergonomics, but they attribute ergonomics to the feel and action of the pipette tip in their hand and not with the tip itself.

Although scientists confirmed that they are inundated with marketing messages, we still discovered that messages about pipetting performance do not actually register with most scientists because they believe that achieving good performance is highly user-dependent.

This is when the conversations became interesting.

Most of our respondents believed that the user needs to know how to pipette properly to achieve good pipetting results. While we agree, we probed further. Specifically, we asked whether it is possible for a manufacturer to re-engineer a pipetting system or a tip to reduce or eliminate user dependencies. Respondents often paused after we asked this question. They were contemplating this notion. Through the ensuing conversation, several expressed surprise that companies had not taken this approach.

However, the true trigger in our conversations manifested when we asked about possible contamination. Scientists have no idea if their pipette is contaminated and proceed on faith that they (or in many cases someone else in their lab) have not accidentally contaminated their pipette through over-suction or splashing of the liquid from the tip into the permanent components of the pipette itself. They also have no way to know or to test whether a pipette is contaminated and merely clean their pipettes each month or so and hope for the best. We found this shocking. Once we had broached this topic, the scientists themselves expressed shock at their own workflows and that they have no way to tell whether the very instrument that touches practically every drop of sample in virtually every experiment in science may at any time be contaminated.

The Full Story

In synthesizing the three sides of the truth, we derived two powerful and actionable insights from our research:

> We can challenge the notion of user dependencies for pipette performance.
>
> Pipette contamination is a mystery—a rather disgusting one, too!

CREATING THE BACKBONE OF THE STORY

Positioning Biotix

Synthesizing the three sides of the truth about the market for pipette tips, we crafted a strong positioning strategy for Biotix that was a unique and refreshing angle within the vast sea of sameness that this market experienced.

Formal Positioning Statement

For scientists and laboratory workers

Who need absolute confidence about the accuracy and purity of their samples during the liquid handling process

Biotix's extensive line of pipette tips

Provides reductions in user-introduced variance through minimizing hanging droplets and incomplete liquid dispensation,

Unlike other pipette tips that open the risk of contamination,

Only Biotix tips alert the user of possible contamination.

We distilled the positioning and these insights into a value proposition synopsis that captured the essence of what Biotix provides to the market:

Value Proposition

Biotix pipette tips reduce user errors in pipetting.

While in a prior chapter we had discovered the great pride that scientists take in their artisanship and in mentoring the younger generations of scientists, we did not find any noble or romantic notion of artisanship when it came to the threat of contamination of their experiments.

We knew we had a strong story. We now needed to architect an elegant experience for laboratory workers to see all of the poor habits that they were forced into due to poor product design.

BUILDING THE STORY: THE CONTENT-CENTRIC MESSAGING STRATEGY

How do you build a story about a piece of plastic and expect engagement by a highly technical audience? Indeed, this is a question that I am often asked when describing the Content-Centric Marketing Model for Science and Healthcare. It is easier to see how the model applies to a technical topic. It is far more difficult to see how to apply it effectively to a non-technical product offering to a technical audience, yet it is just as powerful in both contexts.

In reality, the model has little to do with the technical nature of the product, but rather about the technical nature of the audience and their decision journey. This is a universal template for influencing decisions for products as technical, complicated and expensive as an MRI machine or as non-technical, simple and inexpensive as a pipette tip. In such cases, we must develop provocative Leadership Messaging and arresting Educational materials that are demonstrative of the issues and predispose an audience to be open to receiving a strong Persuasion message that validates the assertion made with Leadership content.

PHASE	RECOGNITION	EXPLORATION	EVALUATION
	Leadership	Education	Persuasion
MESSAGE	Achieving good pipetting performance does not need to be so user dependent.	Better product design can save useless and potentially damaging pipetting habits.	Biotix pipette tips reduce user errors in pipetting.
NARRATIVE	Scientists have been trained to employ good pipetting practices to achieve better precision and accuracy in pipetting. Many of these habits are unnecessary and may be due to lack of product design.	Better-engineered products may eliminate user dependencies and user errors. A better product design would at once improve accuracy, hygiene and ergonomics. Your science is too valuable to risk contamination and inaccurate pipetting.	Having redesigned the pipette tip, Biotix tips alert you when you may have contamination, eliminate wrist-twist by eliminating the need for 'touch-off,' require significantly less force for attaching and detaching the tip and the pipette, and improve performance by eliminating film residues and hanging droplets.

We engineered the narrative to expose the orthodoxies that scientists have adopted out of sheer habit without even realizing it. The goal of the narrative was to reveal these habits in a visceral way so the next time audiences were pipetting, they would become highly aware of their habits and question the necessity of every maneuver. By creating this level of habit awareness, we hoped to create negative associations with their current practices and recognize that they have a need to explore other product choices.

We decided to leverage a powerful pattern in human behavior of mirroring in order to mimic the motions of pipetting.[72] To be successful, our campaign needed to be highly illustrative. The challenge in this campaign was gaining engagement. Instructional content about pipetting practices are everywhere and would be ignored. We needed to go above and beyond.

THE MIRACLE OF CREATIVE: DEMONSTRATING THE MESSAGE

A good creative director knows how to engage audiences. An exceptional creative director knows how to bypass cognitive roadblocks in order to shortcut to a decision. Through our situation analysis and our synthesis, we were confident in the strength of our messaging strategy and our ability to create a Catalytic Experience that shifted the audiences' understanding about pipetting. However, we knew that the challenge with this campaign would lie in engineering and building a robust digital infrastructure to bypass those cognitive roadblocks and escort the audience through their decision journey.

To gain mass exposure and to overcome the high cost of traditional advertising channels to reach audiences, we decided to focus on Facebook as our main outbound channel. With over 1 billion people using this social media platform on a single day,[73] the question is no longer whether social media provides science and medical companies the opportunity to engage technical audiences. The question is how.

---

[72]"Mirroring (psychology)." Wikipedia. Accessed online on March 8, 2016, at en.wikipedia.org/wiki/Mirroring_(psychology).
[73]Facebook. "Company Info." Accessed online on February 29, 2016, at newsroom.fb.com/company-info/.

PHASE	RECOGNITION	EXPLORATION	EVALUATION
INVOKING	CREATIVITY	HYPOTHESIS	VALIDATION
	Leadership	Education	Persuasion
MESSAGE	Achieving good pipetting performance does not need to be so user dependent.	Better product design can save useless and potentially damaging pipetting habits.	Biotix pipette tips reduce user errors in pipetting.
OBJECTIVES	Challenge the orthodoxies of as many scientists as possible to recognize that they are employing bad pipetting habits.	Demonstrate how better product design can eliminate user dependencies on achieving good pipetting results.	Maximize the ease for audiences to move through the final stages of their consideration cycles.
BARRIERS	Reaching many thousands of people using traditional marketing channels will be cost-prohibitive.	Few people will engage with content about pipetting.	Audiences cannot purchase directly through Biotix due to distributor relationships, which cause barriers between the final consideration and purchasing.
STRATEGY	Deploy the campaign through social media and create content that is enticing to share.	Leverage humor to maximize the entertainment value of the content.	Develop a more robust company website that drives the entire decision-making cycle.
SOLUTION	Partner with scientific audience aggregators on Facebook to generate mass exposure and humanize the brand.	Deploy a series of fun videos that demonstrate side-by-side comparisons between conventional and Biotix tips.	Create an interactive product selection guide and work with VWR to connect the specified product directly to its ordering system.

THE CATALYTIC EXPERIENCE—LEVERAGING STORYTELLING

Given the dynamics of Facebook, we needed to create a Catalytic Experience that was irresistibly entertaining and bold. With full awareness of how utterly boring the subject matter of these videos would be, as well as audience propensities to engage in entertainment on social media, we knew we had to go over the top. By employing subtle sarcasm and humor, we developed a series of videos that compared the performance of ordinary tips with Biotix tips.

1. LEADERSHIP—OUTBOUND

We created four episodes of "Tip Tips! From Biotix," each focusing on a design flaw of traditional pipette tips that results in unnecessary pipetting habits. Our two main characters—Piper and Tippen—humorously competed with each other to achieve better pipetting results. While each video became the central content for the Education phase, we created short teasers to use as provocative Leadership messages.

We shared the teaser videos on Facebook through the publisher *The Scientist* (which, as of this writing, has nearly 1.9M followers on its main Facebook page[74]) to gain maximum exposure. We released each video teaser several weeks apart in order to take full advantage of Facebook's social magnification.

We wrote equally funny and bold posts to augment the Leadership message text and call-to-action that accompanied each teaser video. For example, for the teaser video that illustrated the physical force required to attach a conventional tip to a pipette, we wrote "Just how hard do you have to pound to pick up a d@%n pipette tip? Allow Piper and Tippen to demonstrate." We designed each episode to personify the brand, demonstrate the Leadership message and entice the largest number of scientists to click and watch the entire video.

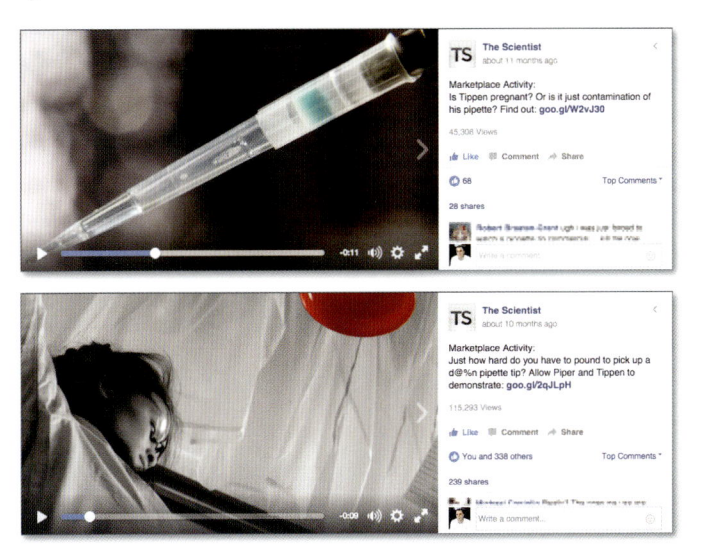

CATALYTIC EXPERIENCES | 141

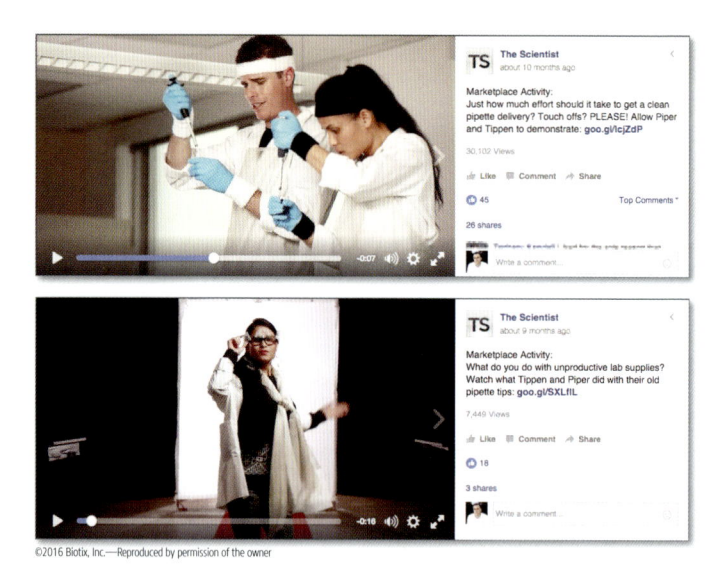

FIGURE 07.02 *The Scientist* magazine's Facebook presence offered the potential to reach 1.9M users, so we placed 10-15 second teasers on its Facebook page over a two-month period. Each teaser included highly provocative messages.[74]

2. EDUCATION—INBOUND

As mentioned, the full-length episodes (approximately 2 minutes each) served as the campaign's main Education content. After demonstrating that good pipetting results need not be as user dependent, every video ended with the line that drove the core of the Education message home: "Remember. It's not the user. It's the tip." Upon viewing these videos, we believed that audiences with whom the need resonated would form their own hypothesis that a better pipette tip would increase their pipetting performance, decrease their chances of contamination and cause less wear and tear on their bodies.

The most efficient way for us to control the audience's decision journey was to host the videos directly on Biotix's main website. We redesigned the entire website to improve the user experience. We simplified it to create a long-scrolling home page that took audiences through their decision journey in just one visit.

---

[74] Facebook. "The Scientist Magazine page." Accessed online on March 12, 2016, at www.facebook.com/TheScientistMagazine.

Leveraging the insight we had gained through our situation analysis—that contamination is a mystery for scientists—we animated the moisture-sensitive dye that alerts users to potential contamination. Our short animation, a critical differentiator and main website headline, served as the main pivot points between the Education and Persuasion stages of the decision journey.

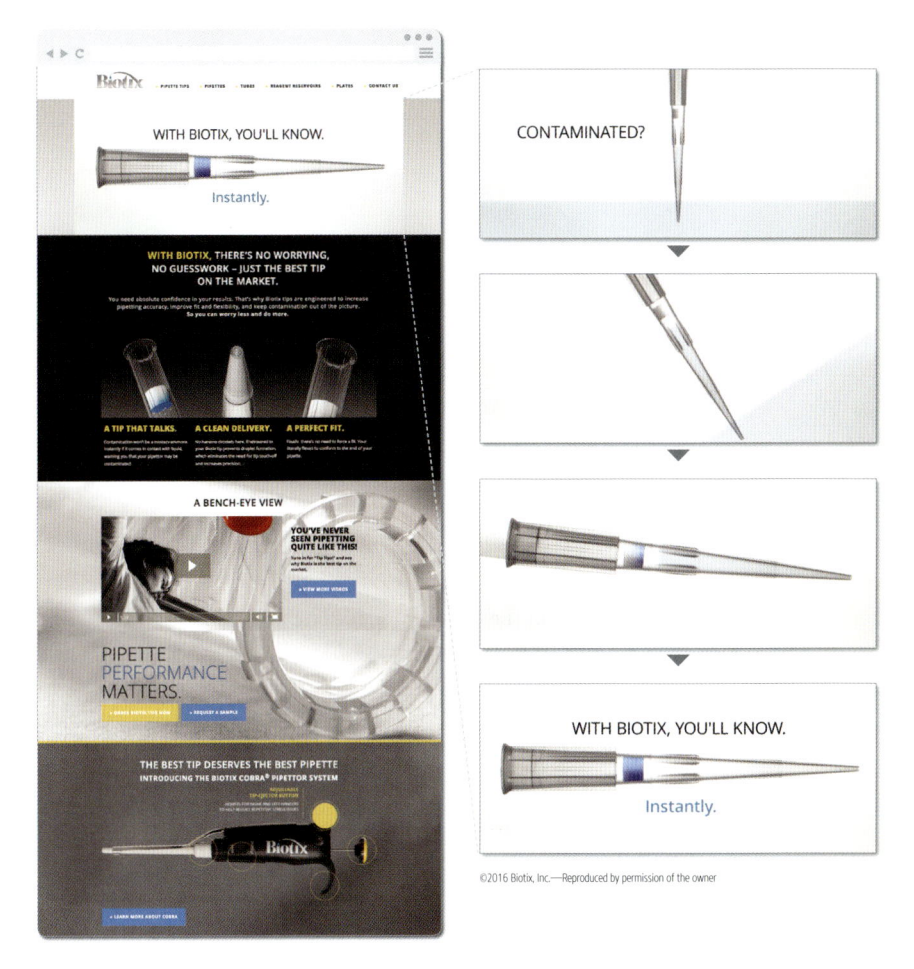

FIGURE 07.03   The marquee animation at the opening experience of the Biotix website clearly demonstrates the most significant question that scientists cannot answer today with their current pipetting systems. This clearly sets the tone for the entire website experience.[75]

---

[75] Accessed online on March 12, 2016, at www.biotix.com. The Biotix logo is a registered trademark of Biotix, Inc. All copyrights of materials belong to Biotix, Inc. Reprinted by permission.

CATALYTIC EXPERIENCES | 143

4. PERSUASION—TRANSACTION

The Biotix website was designed to drive visitors toward transaction, yet the inability to complete the transaction due to the company's relationship with distributors created a major barrier to success. In an online world where nearly 70% of optimized shopping cart experiences are abandoned,[76] Biotix could not afford to lose control of its audience at such a critical moment.

Fortunately the company's main distributor, VWR International, agreed with this notion and allowed us to create a product selector on the Biotix site. This would seamlessly create the correct shopping cart item on the distributor's site.

Figure 07.04 shows our four-step product selection wizard. Every branch point within the product-selection process presented an opportunity to deliver the unique features of the Biotix Pipette Tip in a differentiated and desirable way.

---

[76]Baymard Institute. "33 Cart Abandonment Rate Statistics." Accessed online on March 12, 2016, at baymard.com/lists/cart-abandonment-rate.

FIGURE 07.04 Upon selecting the clear call-to-action "Order Biotix Tips Now," users are presented with an easy, four-step wizard to select their desired products. Small usability considerations can be extremely powerful persuaders. For example, the option to "Print for your purchasing agent" after the user has completed the wizard selection process is persuasive on a subconscious level.[77]

[77]Accessed online on March 12, 2016, at www.biotix.com.

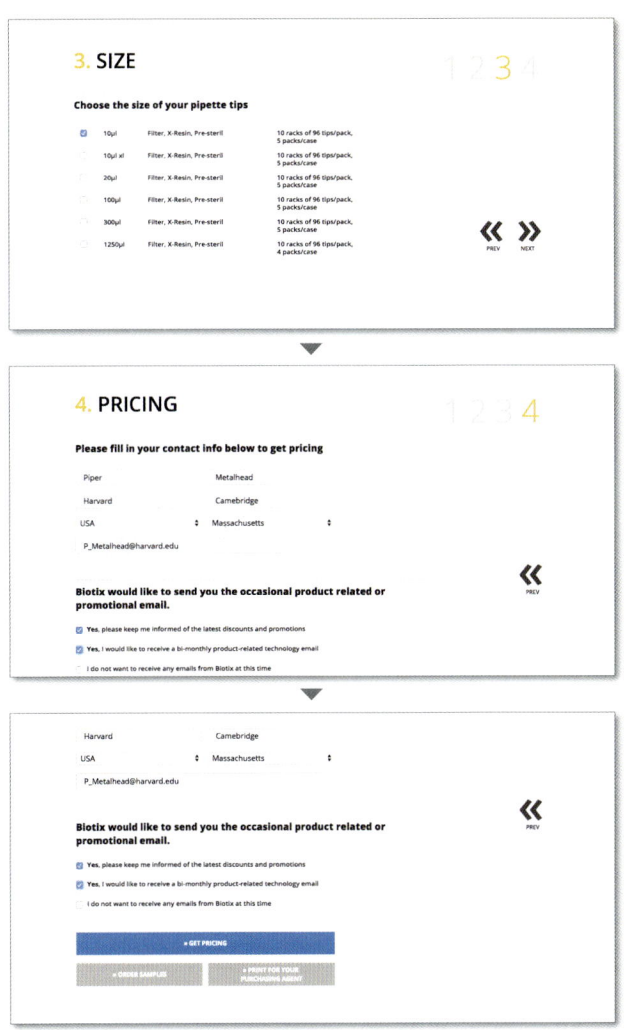

The Biotix product selector was the first-ever instance of any original equipment manufacturer creating a direct path to the shopping cart of VWR, directly ushering its audience to the point of sale and capturing detailed leads in the process.

THE OUTCOME

During the initial six-week period when we launched the four episodes of "Tip Tips" on Facebook, we received an overwhelming engagement level of nearly 200,000 views of the four teaser videos. This exposure translated to a 267% increase in the page views of the Biotix.com website from the average monthly traffic.

Over 3,000 people watched the full episodes of the "Tip Tips" videos on the Biotix website, and over 3,600 engaged with the product selector.

The table below illustrates the key metrics for each phase of the campaign.

PERFORMANCE FOR EACH PHASE

LEADERSHIP		EDUCATION		PERSUASION	
1. Views of the teaser videos 2. Drive traffic to website		1. Website sessions 2. Full episode video views		1. Engagement with product selector 2. Opportunities captured	
Total Impressions	1,293,544	Unique Page Views	36,170	Product Selector Sessions	859
Total Teaser Video Views	195,973	Sessions (Visits)	13,528		
Total Comments	95	Users (Unique Visitors)	11,020	Unique Leads Captured	338
Total 'Likes'	1,201				
Total Shares	298	Total Full Episode Views	3,028		

FIGURE 07.05 The main metrics we measured for Leadership content included brand impressions and numbers of viewers driven to consume the Education content on the Biotix website and, ultimately, to evaluate the product through the transactional tool that we built.

For the first time, Biotix had complete visibility into every step of its marketing efforts. All tactics were quantifiable and the company's marketing had systematized its marketing efforts.

As we analyzed the results of the first six weeks of the new campaign, we could see which parts of the funnel performed well and which parts needed strengthening. More importantly, we now had a robust conversion ratio for each step of the Biotix website to determine how many opportunities would be created.

Biotix is on a mission. By devoting itself to what seems like a small detail, it is making a positive impact in the lives of scientists everywhere. With a systematic digital marketing engine, the brand has the potential to be known across the industry.

CLOSING

A New Question

What Lies Beyond the Horizon?

We live in an exciting time. Never before has so much capability been within our reach. The speed and ease with which we can spin up a campaign, create content and reach our audience is unprecedented today and getting faster and easier yet. But such ease will continue to create noise, and audiences will continue to turn away and turn off.

New communications technologies continue to sweep the landscape. Interactive experiences transform into 'immersive' experiences as virtual or augmented reality becomes mainstream, first inflating expectations but slowly finding their true utility in our professional and personal lives.

As marketers, our path to success is increasingly dependent on technology. We spend more of our time understanding and implementing technologies[78] that promise a utopian future with detailed, actionable marketing metrics.

The rate of change is formidable, and can seem daunting to many; by the time we get used to a reality, the world shifts. What is a

---

[78] S. Brinker. L. McLellan. "The Rise of the Chief Marketing Technologist." *Harvard Business Review*, July-August 2014. Accessed online on March 27, 2016, at hbr.org/2014/07/the-rise-of-the-chief-marketing-technologist.

smart marketer to do in the face of such rapid change? How will marketing science and healthcare be affected by these technology shifts? How can you stay ahead, rather than just staying afloat?

What lies beyond the horizon?

By reading this book, it is my sincere hope that you are now in a better vantage point to answer this question about your own market. In the preceding pages, we have explored how to create a strong, underlying foundation for your digital marketing practice that focuses on the psychology and behavior of scientists and clinicians, so that you can confidently transcend novelty and technology shifts, and instead focus on creating your own long-term vision and implementing it to make meaningful connections with your audience, no matter what lies beyond the horizon.

BE BOLD. GO BIG.

ACKNOWLEDGEMENTS
In Sincere Gratitude

This book is dedicated to all of the people who have taught and inspired me in a myriad of ways.

I thank every member of the Linus team, a group of brilliant, passionate people whom I have had the honor to serve. Nothing would be possible without their amazing capacity to create experiences that connect humans with science in novel ways. They teach me so much about marketing, leadership and being a better person. I am especially indebted to Joanna, whose provocative question led me to articulate my mission, and to Michael, who has authored many of the concepts in this book.

I am grateful for the professionals in our industry who pour their hearts and souls in pushing the boundaries of marketing science and healthcare every day, and for those with whom we have had the privilege to work. Everything I have learned in my career has stemmed from collaborations. I thank all of our clients, who share with us some of their toughest commercialization challenges, giving us the opportunity to advance our thinking and to further their success.

Many mentors have shown me the way and have been patient with me through all of the growing up that I have had to do. To name every person would fill more pages than this entire book. I am especially thankful for Ruby Gadelrab, who is a true visionary, Jim Ellard and Randy Scott, who are exemplars of authentic leadership, and David Weber, who teaches me about bringing sales and marketing closer together.

I am inspired by my friend Mark O'Brien in more ways that I can distill. I owe so much to my dear friend David Haugaard, who has walked with me through dark and light, and to my wife Rebecca, who has shared this journey with me.

Every day, every night, and with every breath in between, I am grateful for Ada.